KNITTING
FOR THE **OUTDOORS**

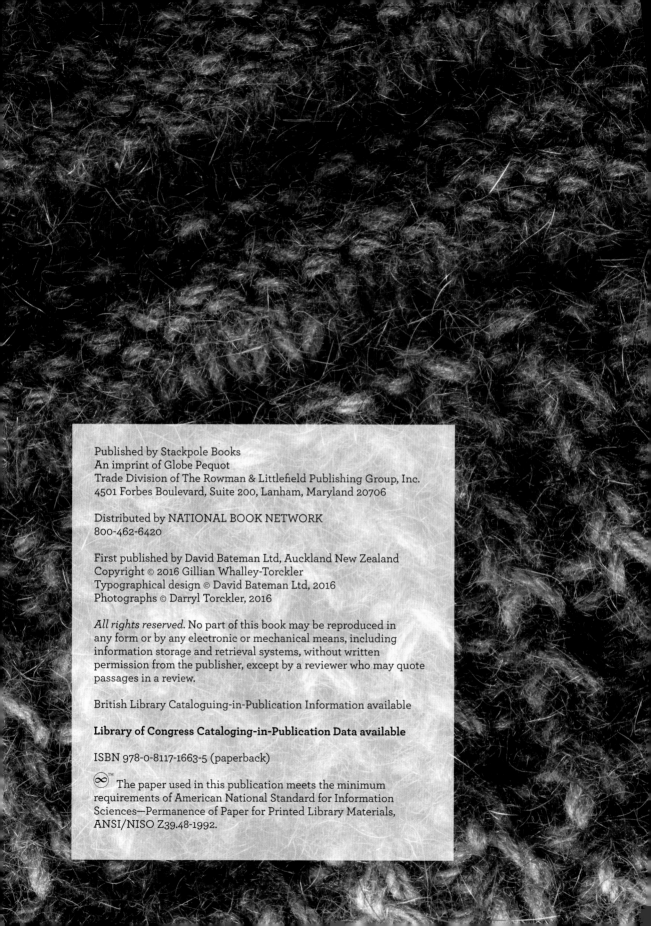

Published by Stackpole Books
An imprint of Globe Pequot
Trade Division of The Rowman & Littlefield Publishing Group, Inc.
4501 Forbes Boulevard, Suite 200, Lanham, Maryland 20706

Distributed by NATIONAL BOOK NETWORK
800-462-6420

First published by David Bateman Ltd, Auckland New Zealand
Copyright © 2016 Gillian Whalley-Torckler
Typographical design © David Bateman Ltd, 2016
Photographs © Darryl Torckler, 2016

British Library Cataloguing-in-Publication Information available

Library of Congress Cataloging-in-Publication Data available

ISBN 978-0-8117-1663-5 (paperback)

♾™ The paper used in this publication meets the minimum
requirements of American National Standard for Information
Sciences—Permanence of Paper for Printed Library Materials,
ANSI/NISO Z39.48-1992.

30 MERINO HANDKNITS FOR
ACTIVE GUYS AND GALS

KNITTING
FOR THE OUTDOORS

GILLIAN WHALLEY-TORCKLER

PHOTOGRAPHY **DARRYL TORCKLER**

STACKPOLE
BOOKS
Guilford, Connecticut

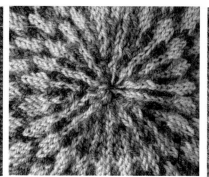

ACKNOWLEDGEMENTS

Special thanks to all my willing models: Creed Bell, Mitchell Davies, Manon Duchampt, Matthew Dyer, Jessamy Jones, Estelle Louie, Justin Swanepoel, Monique Swanepoel, Peter Torckler and Tina Yu — you have made my garments look fantastic. Thanks also to Susi and Peter Thompson who graciously hosted us during our Queenstown shoot and Melitta Swanepoel for her support with models and styling for the forest shoot.

I am indebted to the wonderful and patient publishing team at David Bateman in Auckland: Tracey Borgfeldt and Paul Bateman for the opportunity to create this book; Caroline List, who has patience beyond belief and never complained once when she should have. And Shelley Watson of Sublime Design for the design work.

Thanks to Jennifer Kipfer for casting her experienced knitter's eyes over the patterns and Sally Dunbier for final proofreading, although any mistakes that remain are entirely my own. Thanks to my agent, Frances Plumpton, with whom coffee is long overdue now that this book is complete!

I would also like to thank the yarn manufacturers who donated their sumptuous yarn for me to work with — Australian Country Spinners, Lion Brand, Naturally Yarns, The Rare Yarns Company, Skeinz, Touch Yarns, Zealana — and ChiaGoo for their equally wonderful needles.

Finally, thanks to my wonderful family, who have been extremely patient during the production of this book. Last but not least, enormous thanks to my extraordinary husband who has taken all of the beautiful photographs in this book. I feel lucky to have such marvellous people supporting me.

Gillian

CONTENTS

INTRODUCTION

This book has been a wonderful journey on which I was motivated to knit outdoor garments that would be both functional and fashionable. And I wanted to create designs that would look great on both men and women. There are hats, scarves, gloves and sleeveless vests to suit almost any occasion or activity and most are unisex.

When my publishers requested that all of the garments in this book be made of merino wool, I agreed willingly. Merino, with its fine fiber, is this knitter's dream yarn. Some of the patterns in this book are crafted from pure merino yarns; others use merino blended with fibers such as alpaca, possum and angora. All are divinely soft to wear and to work with. I must admit that in the past, being eternally budget-conscious, I have shied away from the slightly higher expense of merino yarns. Now, I am pleased to say, I am cured of that stinginess! Merino is always worth the investment.

Throughout the book, I have used circular needles for many patterns. This allows you to create garments without side seams and to knit some of the scarves across, rather than lengthwise. If you are new to circulars, then I encourage you to embrace them. I have a set of ChiaoGoo interchangeable needles that I carry everywhere. For a small upfront investment, I have all the needles (in different sizes and lengths) I need at my fingertips.

The patterns in this book rely on yarn texture and needle size to obtain the correct structure. Do please check your tension. I have included a list of yarns used at the back of the book and all of these were available at the time of printing. When substituting yarns, start with the yarn weight, suggested needle size and take into account the yardage. If your chosen yarn matches then you should have success.

I hope you love making and wearing these outdoor knits as much as I have loved creating them. If you feel like sharing your creations, you can find me on ravelry.com (GillianNZ) or my website gilliantorckler.com. I would love to see your own projects.

One of the unanticipated pleasures of working with luxury merino yarns has been the yarn descriptions themselves — I have been knitting with colors such as Black Velvet (black), Tattoo Me Topaz (blue), Green With Envy (lime green) and Pale Primrose (off white). The makers of these yarns have had creative fun naming them and I have had great fun creating with these colors too. Color is important to me — in life and craft. I have used natural palettes but also bright clean colors, and I have mixed colors to create interesting effects. I encourage you to experiment with color. Outdoor knits don't have to be drab.

Happy knitting!
Gillian

USEFUL KNITTING TIPS

These tips may be helpful when knitting some of the patterns in this book:

KNITTING IN THE ROUND:

After you have cast on (and this applies to both double-pointed and circular needles) you need to make sure that the stitches are not twisted around on the needles before you start knitting the first round, otherwise you will end up with a twist in the work. Lay the needles on a table and check that the cast on edges are all lying flat and on the insides of the needles.

NO-SEW SEAMS:

This method gives a more even finish and is great for shoulder seams, but can be used anywhere two rows meet. When you get to the end of the row, do not bind off. Instead, leave the stitches on the needles for both of the pieces of knitting that you want to join. With right sides facing, hold the two needles parallel to each other in one hand. Using a third needle, knit two stitches (one from each needle) together, then bind off as usual.

USING MARKERS:

Markers can be very useful for keeping track of where you are when working in the round. Place a marker at the end of the first round and slip it with every subsequent round you complete.

IN THE FOREST

DESIGNED FOR ACTION

GO ANYWHERE WOMAN'S VEST

Knitted in the round and flat   Level: Advanced

This very simple pattern features a textured fabric that is created by needlework alone, using three shades of the same yarn; you have to use three colors for the pattern to work. This striking yarn is a pure merino one that feels 'polished' and almost like a cotton yarn. As a result, the individual stitches and yarns remain distinct from one another. This vest would look great with a pair of jeans, or paired with a black outfit for the evening.

FINISHED MEASUREMENTS:

Small: 32 in (81.25 cm) chest, 26 in (66 cm) waist

Medium: 34 in (86.25 cm) chest, 28 in (71 cm) waist

Large: 36 in (91.5 cm) chest, 30 in (76 cm) waist

Extra-large: 38 in (96.5 cm) chest, 32 in (81.25 cm) waist

YARN:

Australian Superfine Merino DK by Cleckheaton

100% superfine merino; 2.29 oz (65 g) skein; 142 yds (130 m)

Contrast Color 1 (CC1) 3 (3, 4, 4) skeins: shade #65 Mustard

Contrast Color 2 (CC2) 1 (1, 2, 2) skein(s): shade #36 Dark Grape

Contrast Color 3 (CC3) 1 (1, 2, 2) skein(s): shade #59 Pale Primrose

NEEDLES:

US 6 (4 mm) and US 3 (3.25 mm) straight needles and US 3 (3.25 mm) approximately 16 in (40 cm) circular needle

GAUGE:

Using US 6 (4 mm) needles, 24 stitches x 40 rows = 4 in (10 cm) over pattern. Adjust the needle size as needed to get the correct tension.

To start, using CC1 cast on 144 (156, 168, 180) stitches with US 3 (3.25 mm) circular needle:

Start working in the round, place a marker, if using, and slip on every round. Do not turn the needles at the end of the round, just keep going in the same direction, with the right side facing you.

Round 1: *k1tbl, p1*, repeat from *to* to the end of the round.

Repeat this round until work measures 7 in (17.75 cm).

Change to US 6 (4 mm) straight needles to divide for the front and back, creating the overlaps at the sides as you go:

For the front: using one straight needle, knit 11 stitches but do not drop the loops as you normally would to complete the stitch; transfer the loops to the right-hand needle of the circular needle (so you are effectively turning one stitch into two). Knit the next 76 (82, 88, 94) stitches normally, then knit the next 11 stitches, again transferring the loops to the circular needle, as above. You should have 98 (104, 110, 116) stitches for the front section. Slip these stitches onto a stitch holder.

For the back: adjust the stitches on the circular needle so the loops of the 11 stitches already worked for the front, as above, are located on each side of the remaining 46 (52, 58, 64) stitches. Using a straight needle, knit these 11 stitches, then knit the next 46 (52, 58, 64) stitches, then knit the remaining 11 stitches already worked for the front. You should have 68 (74, 80, 86) stitches for the back section.

Work both the front and back according to the following pattern. The front is wider to account for the overlap at the sides, otherwise both are alike, except for the number of stitches.

Add in the contrast colors to begin the pattern:

Pattern row 1 (CC1): *k1, yf, sl1 and carry yarn across front of slipped stitch, yb*, repeat from *to* to the last stitch, p1.

Pattern row 2 (CC2): *yf, sl1 and carry yarn across front of slipped stitch, yb, k1*, repeat from *to* to the last stitch, p1.

Pattern row 3 (CC3): *k1, yf, sl1 and carry yarn across front of slipped stitch, yb*, repeat from *to* to the last stitch, p1.

Pattern row 4 (CC1): *yf, sl1 and carry yarn across front of slipped stitch, yb, k1*, repeat from *to* to the last stitch, p1.

Pattern row 5 (CC2): *k1, yf, sl1 and carry yarn across front of slipped stitch, yb*, repeat from *to* to the last stitch, p1.

Pattern row 6 (CC3): *yf, sl1 and carry yarn across front of slipped stitch, yb, k1*, repeat from *to* to the last stitch, p1.

These 6 rows form the pattern. You should start to see it emerge after 6–12 rows. Repeat these 6 rows until both the front and back measure:

Small: 11½ in (29.25 cm) from start of pattern.

Medium: 12 in (30.5 cm) from start of pattern.

Large: 12½ in (31.75 cm) from start of pattern.

Extra-large: 13 in (33 cm) from start of pattern.

To finish the neckline:

Front: work 13 stitches in pattern, bind off the next 72 (78, 84, 90) stitches loosely knitwise, work 13 stitches in pattern.

Back: work 13 stitches in pattern, bind off the next 42 (48, 54, 60) stitches loosely knitwise, work 13 stitches in pattern.

To make the shoulder seams:

Transfer the 13 stitches from the right back and right front to 2 straight needles. With right sides together, hold these needles side by side and using a third needle, pick up and knit one stitch from each needle together. At the same time, loosely bind off the stitches knitwise. Repeat for the left shoulder.

To finish the armholes, using US 3 (3.25 mm) circular needle, pick up and knit 112 (118, 126, 130) stitches along the side edge:

Round 1: *k1tbl, p1*, repeat from *to* to the end of the round. Place marker, if using, and slip every round.

Round 2: *k1tbl, p1*, repeat from *to* to the end of the round.

Round 3 (decrease): sl1, k1, psso, *k1tbl, p1*, repeat from *to* to last 2 stitches, k2tog (110, 116, 124, 128 stitches).

Round 4 (decrease): sl1, k1, psso, *k1tbl, p1*, repeat from *to* to last 2 stitches, k2tog (108, 114, 122, 126 stitches).

Round 5 (decrease): sl1, k1, psso, *k1tbl, p1*, repeat from *to* to last 2 stitches, k2tog (106, 112, 120, 124 stitches).

Round 6 (decrease): sl1, k1, psso, *k1tbl, p1*, repeat from *to* to last 2 stitches, k2tog (104, 110, 118, 122 stitches).

Round 7: bind off loosely in k1, p1 rib.

Repeat for the other armhole.

TO FINISH

Break off yarn leaving an 8 in (20 cm) tail and tie off securely. Using a darning needle, weave yarn tails into stitches on the wrong side.

INFINITE DIAMONDS SCARF

Knitted flat | Level: Intermediate

This classic scarf features a geometric diamond pattern with a fluted edge composed of a series of recurring cables. I have used a lovely cream merino, but you can make it in any solid color you choose. I do think it is best crafted in a solid color to show off the pattern detail. Perhaps a subtle tweed colorway could work — nothing too dramatic though, as you don't want to detract from your beautiful stitchwork. The photographed scarf is fairly long, but you can easily adjust the pattern to any length you prefer.

FINISHED MEASUREMENTS:

The scarf is 85 in (216 cm) in length and 9 in (22.75 cm) wide

YARN:

Touch Merino 8 ply/DK

100% merino yarn; 1.76 oz (50 g) skein; 109 yds (100 m)

5 skeins: shade #216

NEEDLES:

US 5 (3.75 mm) straight needles, plus cable needle

GAUGE:

Using US 5 (3.75 mm) needles, 18 stitches x 28 rows = 4 in (10 cm) over garter stitch pattern (inside of the diamonds). Adjust the needle size as needed to get the correct tension.

To start, cast on 45 stitches with US 5 (3.75 mm) straight needles:

Row 1: k5, *p5, k5*, repeat from *to* to the end.

Row 2: p5, *k5, p5*, repeat from *to* to the end.

These 2 rows form the basis of a wide rib pattern. Repeat these rows until work measures approximately 5 in (12.75 cm) ending with row 2.

Begin pattern:

Row 1: k20, k2tog, yo, k1, yo, sl1, k1, psso, k20.

Row 2: p21, k3, p21.

Row 3 (cable row): sl5 onto cn, hold cn at back, k5, k5 from cn, k9, k2tog, yo, k3, yo, sl1, k1, psso, k9, sl5 onto cn, hold cn at front, k5, k5 from cn.

Row 4: p20, k5, p20.

Row 5: k18, k2tog, yo, k5, yo, sl1, k1, psso, k18.

Row 6: p19, k7, p19.

Row 7: k17, k2tog, yo, k7, yo, sl1, k1, psso, k17.

Row 8: p18, k9, p18.

Row 9 (cable row): sl5 onto cn, hold cn at back, k5, k5 from cn, k6, k2tog, yo, k9, yo, sl1, k1, psso, k6, sl5 onto cn, hold cn at front, k5, k5 from cn.

Row 10: p17, k11, p17.

Row 11: k15, k2tog, yo, k11, yo, sl1, k1, psso, k15.

Row 12: p16, k13, p16.

Row 13: k14, k2tog, yo, k13, yo, sl1, k1, psso, k14.

Row 14: p15, k15, p15.

Row 15 (cable row): sl5 onto cn, hold cn at back, k5, k5 from cn, k3, k2tog, yo, k15, yo, sl1, k1, psso, k3, sl5 onto cn, hold cn at front, k5, k5 from cn.

Row 16: p14, k17, p14.

Row 17: k12, k2tog, yo, k17, yo, sl1, k1, psso, k12.

Row 18: p13, k19, p13.

Row 19: k11, k2tog, yo, k19, yo, sl1, k1, psso, k11.

Row 20: p12, k21, p12.

Row 21 (cable row): sl5 onto cn, hold cn at back, k5, k5 from cn, k2tog, yo, k21, yo, sl1, k1, psso, sl5 onto cn, hold cn at front, k5, k5 from cn.

Row 22: p11, k23, p11.

Row 23: k11, yo, sl1, k1, psso, k19, k2tog, yo, k11.

Row 24: p12, k21, p12.

Row 25: k12, yo, sl1, k1, psso, k17, k2tog, yo, k12.

Row 26: p13, k19, p13.

Row 27 (cable row): sl5 onto cn, hold cn at back, k5, k5 from cn, k3, yo, sl1, k1, psso, k15, k2tog, yo, k3, sl5 onto cn, hold cn at front, k5, k5 from cn.

Row 28: p14, k17, p14.

Row 29: k14, yo, sl1, k1, psso, k13, k2tog, yo, k14.

Row 30: p15, k15, p15.

Row 31: k15, yo, sl1, k1, psso, k11, k2tog, yo, k15.

Row 32: p16, k13, p16.

Row 33 (cable row): sl5 onto cn, hold cn at back, k6, yo, sl1, k1, psso, k9, k2tog, yo, k6, sl5 onto cn, hold cn at front, k5, k5 from cn.

Row 34: p17, k11, p17.

Row 35: k17, yo, sl1, k1, psso, k7, k2tog, yo, k17.

Row 36: p18, k9, p18.

Row 37: k18, yo, sl1, k1, psso, k5, k2tog, yo, k18.

Row 38: p19, k7, p19.

Row 39 (cable row): sl5 onto cn, hold cn at back, k5, k5 from cn, k9, yo, sl1, k1, psso, k3, k2tog, yo, k9, sl5 onto cn, hold cn at front, k5, k5 from cn.

Row 40: p20, k5, p20.

Row 41: k20, yo, sl1, k1, psso, k1, k2tog, yo, k20.

Row 42: p21, k3, p21.

Row 43: k21, yo, sl1, k2tog, psso, yo, k21

Row 44: purl.

Repeat rows 1–44 until work measures 80 in (203 cm) ending with row 44.

Work 5 in (12.75 cm) in k5, p5 rib as at the start.

Bind off loosely in rib pattern.

You should have 10 diamond patterns in total. You can adjust the length of the scarf by removing or adding in extra rows, but only do so by adding or subtracting an entire pattern sequence (i.e. rows 1–44).

TO FINISH

Break off yarn leaving an 8 in (20 cm) tail and tie off securely. Using a darning needle, weave yarn tail into stitches on the wrong side.

RUGGED FINGERLESS GLOVES

Knitted in the round   Level: Intermediate

These fingerless gloves have a basket weave pattern across the top that is created through a series of interlocking cables. The wrist section is designed to be extra long so that you can either fold it over, or pull it up to cover the forearms. I have used a very durable merino/possum worsted weight yarn, which makes them soft and warm, yet strong and rugged — ideal for the man in your life!

FINISHED MEASUREMENTS:

Small: 11½ in (29.25 cm) long and 3¼ in (8.25 cm) wide

Medium: 12 in (30.5 cm) long and 4 in (10 cm) wide

Large: 12½ in (31.75 cm) long and 4¾ in (12 cm) wide

YARN:

Zealana Artisan Series Heron/worsted weight

80% fine merino, 20% brushtail possum yarn; 1.76 oz (50 g) skein; 109 yds (100 m)

2 skeins: shade H02 Bottle Green

NEEDLES:

US 7 (4.5 mm) double-pointed needles plus cable needle

GAUGE:

Using US 7 (4.5 mm) needles, 20 stitches x 28 rows = 4 in (10 cm) over k2, p2 rib pattern. Adjust the needle size as needed to get the correct tension.

To start the left-hand glove, cast on 40 (44, 48) stitches with US 7 (4.5 mm) double-pointed needles:

Distribute the stitches evenly across 3 of the needles and start working in the round.

LH round 1: *k2, p2*, repeat from *to* to the end. Repeat this round until work measures 4 (4½, 5) in (10, 11.5, 12.75 cm).

Start cable pattern:

Place marker, if using, and slip on every round.

LH cable round 1: (k2, p2) 4 (5, 6) times, *sl2 onto cn, hold cn at front, (k2, p2) from left-hand needle, k2 from cn, p2*, repeat from *to* to the end of the round. You should have 3 cables.

Repeat LH round 1, 5 times.

LH cable round 2: (k2, p2) 5 (6, 7) times, *sl2 onto cn, hold cn at back, (k2, p2) from left-hand needle, k2 from cn, p2*, repeat from *to* twice, k2, p2. You should have 2 cables.

Repeat LH round 1, 5 times.

Repeat LH cable round 1.

Repeat LH round 1, 5 times.

Repeat LH cable round 2.

Repeat LH round 1, 5 times.

Repeat LH cable round 1.

Stop rib pattern for palm of left hand:

LH round 2: k14 (18, 22), *p2, k2*, repeat from *to* to last 2 stitches, p2.

Repeat LH round 2, 4 times.

LH cable round 3: k14 (18, 22), p2, k2, p2, *sl2 onto cn, hold cn at back, (k2, p2) from left-hand needle, k2 from cn, p2*, repeat from *to* twice, k2, p2.

You should have 2 cables.

Repeat LH round 2, 5 times.

LH cable round 4: k14 (18, 22), p2, *sl2 onto cn, hold cn at front, (k2, p2) from left-hand needle, k2 from cn, p2*, repeat from *to* to the end of the round.

Make hole for left thumb:

LH round 3: k8 (11, 14), cast on 6 (7, 8) stitches, then place the next 6 (7, 8) stitches onto a stitch holder, *p2, k2*, repeat from *to* to the last 2 stitches, p2 (40, 44, 48 stitches).

Repeat LH round 2, 3 times.

Repeat LH cable round 3.

Repeat LH round 2, 5 times.

Repeat LH cable round 4.

Repeat LH round 2, twice.

Bind off loosely knitwise.

To complete thumb, place stitches on the holder back onto needles and pick up and knit 6 (7, 8) stitches along the cast-on edge (12, 14, 16 stitches):

Knit 12 (14, 16) rounds. Bind off loosely knitwise.

To start the right-hand glove, cast on 40 (44, 48) stitches with US 7 (4.5 mm) double-pointed needles:

Distribute the stitches evenly across 3 of the needles and start working in the round.

RH round 1: *k2, p2*, repeat from *to* to the end.

Repeat this round until work measures 4 (4½, 5) in (10, 11.5, 12.75 cm).

Start cable pattern:

Place marker, if using, and slip on every round.

RH cable round 1: k2, p2, *sl2 onto cn, hold cn at front, (k2, p2) from left-hand needle, k2 from cn, p2*, repeat from *to* twice, (k2, p2) to the end of the round. You should have 3 cables.

Repeat RH round 1, 5 times.

RH cable round 2: k2, p2, *sl2 onto cn, hold cn at back, (k2, p2) from left-hand needle, k2 from cn, p2*, repeat from *to* once, k2, p2, (k2, p2) to the end of the round. You should have 2 cables.

Repeat RH round 1, 5 times.

Repeat RH cable round 1.

Repeat RH round 1, 5 times.

Repeat RH cable round 2.

Repeat RH round 1, 5 times.

Repeat RH cable round 1.

Stop rib pattern for palm of right hand:

RH round 2: (k2, p2) 7 times, k12 (16, 20).

Repeat RH round 2, 4 times.

RH cable round 3: (k2, p2) twice *sl2 onto cn, hold cn at back, (k2, p2) from left-hand needle, k2 from cn, p2*, repeat from *to* once more, k2, p2, k16 (20, 24). You should have 2 cables.

Repeat RH round 2, 5 times.

RH cable round 4: k2, p2, *sl2 onto cn, hold cn at front, (k2, p2) from left-hand needle, k2 from cn, p2*, repeat from *to* twice, k14 (18, 20). You should have 3 cables.

Make hole for right thumb:

Repeat RH round 2.

RH round 3: (k2, p2) 7 times, cast on 6 (7, 8) stitches, then place the next 6 (7, 8) stitches onto a stitch holder and knit to the end of the round (40, 44, 48 stitches).

Repeat RH round 2, 3 times.

Repeat RH cable round 3.

Repeat RH round 2, 5 times.

Repeat RH cable round 4.

Repeat RH round 2, twice.

Bind off loosely knitwise.

To complete thumb, place stitches on the holder back onto needles and pick up and knit 6 (7, 8) stitches along the cast-on edge (12, 14, 16 stitches):

Knit 12 (14, 16) rounds.

Bind off loosely knitwise.

TO FINISH

Break off yarn leaving an 8 in (20 cm) tail and tie off securely. Using a darning needle, weave yarn tail into stitches on the wrong side.

CHEVRON BEANIE

Knitted in the round   Level: Intermediate

FINISHED MEASUREMENTS:

The pattern is provided in one size and will fit 20¼ in (51.5 cm) to 23¼ in (59 cm) head circumference.

YARN:

Zealana Artisan Cozi 4 ply

58% merino, 20% nylon, 15% possum, 5% alpaca, 2% elastic nylon; 1.76 oz (50 g) skein; 186 yds (170 m)

Main Color (MC)
1 skein: shade C03 Custard

Contrast Color (CC)
1 skein: shade C01 Sugar

NEEDLES:

US 2 (2.75 mm) set of double-pointed needles.

GAUGE:

Using US 2 (2.75 mm) needles, 30 stitches x 40 rows = 4 in (10 cm) over pattern. Adjust the needle size as needed to get the correct tension.

When I am designing, I like to experiment with yarns and needle sizes. This hat is a prime example of one of those experiments. It is made of sock yarn and the result is a lightweight stretchy cap. It feels so warm, yet weightless. I think the key to this is the blend of fibers — merino, possum, nylon and elastic. This is a finely crafted yarn for the finely crafted cozy hat you are going to make. That the yarn is called 'Cozi' is no coincidence.

To start the hat, using MC, cast on 120 stitches with US 2 (2.75 mm) double-pointed needles:

Distribute the stitches evenly across three of the needles and start working in the round. Do not turn your work. Keep knitting around the circle, with the right side of your work facing you. Place marker, if using, and slip on every round.

Work 4 in (10 cm) in k2, p2 rib.

Last round (increase): *k11, kfb*, repeat from *to* to the end of the round (130 stitches).

Start pattern:

Round 1 (MC): knit.

Round 2 (MC): *sl1, k1, psso, k4, m1, k1, m1, k4, k2tog*, repeat from *to* to the end of the round.

These 2 rounds form the pattern. Change colors as below, always making sure you start with a round 1 when the new color is added.

Work rounds 1 & 2 , 2 times in MC.

Work rounds 1 & 2 , 2 times in CC.

Work rounds 1 & 2 , 3 times in MC.

Work rounds 1 & 2 , 3 times in CC.

Work rounds 1 & 2 , 4 times in MC.

Work rounds 1 & 2 , 4 times in CC.

Work rounds 1 & 2 in MC. Break off MC.

Work rounds 1 & 2, 3 times in CC.

Start decreasing for the crown and continue in CC only:

Round 1: knit.

Round 2: *sl1, k1, psso, k9, k2tog*, repeat from *to* to the end of the round (110 stitches).

Round 3: knit.

Round 4: *sl1, k1, psso, k7, k2tog*, repeat from *to* to the end of the round (90 stitches).

Round 5: knit.

Round 6: *sl1, k1, psso, k5, k2tog*, repeat from *to* to the end of the round (70 stitches).

Round 7: knit.

Round 8: *sl1, k1, psso, k3, k2tog*, repeat from *to* to the end of the round (50 stitches).

Round 9: knit.

Round 10: *sl1, k1, psso, k1, k2tog*, repeat from *to* to the end of the round (30 stitches).

Round 11: knit.

Round 12: *sl1, k2tog, psso*, repeat from *to* to the end of the round (10 stitches).

Break off yarn and pull through the remaining stitches on the needle. Tie off securely.

TO FINISH

Break off yarn leaving an 8 in (20 cm) tail and tie off securely. Using a darning needle, sew through the center a few times, ensuring no gaps remain. Weave yarn tails into stitches on the wrong side.

WEEKEND KHAKI VEST

Knitted flat   Level: Intermediate–Advanced

This pattern starts with the long cable that extends all the way down the front and back, dividing for the neck. Once the cable section is completed, you pick up the side edges and work sideways across the garment, completing both the front and back at the same time. There is a similar women's vest on page 82, but that one is less shaped and has a different cable pattern.

FINISHED MEASUREMENTS:

Small: 37 in (94 cm) chest and 28 in (71 cm) long (from shoulder)

Medium: 41 in (104 cm) chest and 28 in (71 cm) long (from shoulder)

Large: 45 in (114.25 cm) chest and 28 in (71 cm) long (from shoulder)

YARN:

Skeinz Heritage Silver Lining 8 ply

Pure New Zealand rare breed 100% merino yarn; 1.76 oz (50 g) skein; 119 yds (109 m)

Main Color (MC) 6 (7, 8) skeins: shade Ahuriri Green

Contrast Color (CC) 2 (2, 3) skeins: shade Five Mile Bush

NEEDLES:

US 6 (4 mm) straight needles and US 5 (3.75 mm) straight and circular needles at least 24 in (60 cm) long, plus a cable needle

GAUGE:

Using US 5 (3.75 mm) needles, 22 stitches x 28 rows = 4 in (10 cm) over stocking stitch used for the body. Adjust the needle size as needed to get the correct tension.

To start, using MC cast on 26 stitches with US 6 (4 mm) straight needles:

Row 1: (p2, k6) 3 times, p2.

Row 2: (k2, p6) 3 times, k2.

Repeat rows 1 & 2, 4 more times (rows 3–10).

Row 11 (cable row): *p2, sl3 stitches onto cn, hold at back, k3 from left-hand needle, k3 from cn*, repeat from *to* to last 2 stitches, p2.

Row 12: (k2, p6) 3 times, k2.

Row 13: (p2, k6) 3 times, p2.

Row 14: (k2, p6) 3 times, k2.

Repeat rows 13 & 14, 3 more times (rows 15–20).

Repeat rows 11–20, 6 times.

Then repeat the cable row (row 11).

Your work should measure 14 in (35.5 cm) from the cast-on edge. If you want to adjust the length, do so now, but remember this will affect the number of stitches you pick up later for the sides.

Divide for the neck, working on left-hand side:

LH row 1: p2, k6, p2, k3, turn (13 stitches).

Place remaining stitches on a stitch holder and work on these 13 stitches as follows:

LH row 2: p3, k2, p6, k2.

Repeat LH rows 1 & 2, 4 more times (rows 3–10).

LH row 11 (cable row): p2, sl3 stitches onto cn, hold at back, k3 from left-hand needle, k3 from cn, p2, k3.

Repeat LH rows 2–11, 6 times.

Repeat LH rows 2–10, once more. Place stitches on a stitch holder.

Return to right-hand side, rejoin yarn and move the stitches on the holder onto a straight needle with right side facing:

RH row 1: k3, p2, k6, p2, turn (13 stitches).

RH row 2: k2, p6, k2, p3.

Repeat RH rows 1 & 2, 4 more times (rows 3–10).

RH row 11 (cable row): k3, p2, sl3 stitches onto cn, hold at back, k3 from left-hand needle, k3 from cn, p2.

Repeat RH rows 2–11, 6 times.

Repeat RH rows 2–10, once more.

Start working on all 26 stitches again for the back cable:

With right sides facing, place the RH stitches, then the LH stitches, onto a straight needle.

Row 1 (cable row): *p2, sl3 stitches onto cn, hold at back, k3 from left-hand needle, k3 from cn*, repeat from *to* to last 2 stitches, p2.

Row 2: (k2, p6) 3 times, k2.

Row 3: (p2, k6) 3 times, p2.

Repeat rows 2 & 3, 3 more times (rows 4–9).

Row 10: (k2, p6) 3 times, k2.

Repeat rows 1–10, 16 times.

Your work should measure 28 in (71 cm) from the top neck edge of the back (where you rejoined the 2 cable sides). If you have adjusted the front length, remember to adjust the back length by the same amount.

Bind off loosely, knitwise.

To make the sides, using MC and US 5 (3.75 mm) circular needle, with right side facing, pick up and knit 212 (all sizes)

stitches along the edge of the cable piece you have just completed:

You are going to use the circular needle as if it is straight needles — it helps to hold all of the stitches on.

Row 1 (MC): purl.

Row 2 (CC): knit.

Row 3 (CC): purl.

Row 4 (MC): knit.

Row 5 (MC): purl.

Repeat rows 2–5, 4 times.

You should have 5 stripes of CC. Break off CC.

Work 10 (18, 26) rows stocking stitch (1 row knit, 1 row purl) in MC.

Your work should measure 6½ (7½, 8¾) in (16.5, 19, 22.25 cm) from cable edge.

Divide for armhole:

Keeping stocking stitch pattern correct, work 64 stitches, bind off next 84 stitches, work remaining 64 stitches to the end. Place 64 stitches for front on stitch holder.

Continue working on the back section only.

Keep stocking stitch pattern going and decrease 1 stitch every alternate row at the armhole edge until 56 stitches remain by starting each knit row with sl1, k1, psso (16 rows).

Work 4 rows stocking stitch.

Do not bind off, place stitches on a holder.

Join yarn to front section.

Keep stocking stitch pattern going and decrease 1 stitch every alternate row at armhole edge until 56 stitches remain by ending each knit row with k2tog (16 rows).

Work 4 rows stocking stitch. Do not bind off, place stitches on a holder.

To make side seams:

Place the 56 stitches from each stitch holder back onto 2 straight needles. With the right sides together, hold these needles side by side and using a third needle, pick up and knit 1 stitch from each needle together. At the same time, loosely bind off the stitches knitwise.

Repeat for the other side of cable section.

Make the ribbed band, using MC and US 5 (3.75 mm) circular needle:

Starting at the edge of the cable band at the back, pick up and knit 184 stitches along the bottom edge of the garment. Place marker, if using, and slip on every round.

This is a k2, p2 rib pattern except for the cable sections, where the rib is a k6, p2 pattern.

Round 1 (MC): k6, p2, k6, p2, k6, p2, (k2, p2) until the edge of the cable segment on the front, k6, p2, k6, p2, k6, p2, (k2, p2) to the end of the round.

Rounds 2–8 (MC): work 7 more rounds in rib pattern.

Round 9 (CC): knit.

Round 10 (CC): work 1 round in rib pattern.

Round 11 (MC): knit.

Rounds 12–13 (MC): work 2 rounds in rib pattern.

Round 14 (CC): knit.

Rounds 15–21 (CC): work 7 rows in rib pattern.

Round 22 (MC): knit.

Round 23 (MC): Bind off loosely in rib pattern.

To make the ribbed armhole edges, using CC and US 5 (3.75 mm) circular needle:

Starting at the side seam, pick up and knit 100 stitches along the armhole edge of the garment.

Rounds 1–3 (CC): k2, p2.

Round 4 (MC): knit.

Rounds 5–7 (MC): k2, p2.

Round 8 (MC): Bind off loosely in rib pattern.

Repeat for the other armhole.

TO FINISH

Break off yarn leaving an 8 in (20 cm) tail and tie off securely. Using a darning needle, weave yarn tails into stitches on the wrong side.

WARM WOODSMAN HAT

Knitted in the round   Level: Intermediate

This warm hat has an asymmetrical shape, so that the ribbed edge naturally covers the ears. I have used three colors to create the pattern — an earthy green, a deep sea blue and a stone grey. Of course, any color combination would work. The stitch detail adds texture and interest to the main part of the hat and the contrasting edge brings it all together.

FINISHED MEASUREMENTS:

Small–medium: 19–21 in (48.25–53.5 cm).

Medium–large: 22–24 in (55.75–60 cm).

YARN:

Zealana Kauri/worsted weight

60% merino, 30% brushtail possum, 10% mulberry silk; 1.76 oz (50 g) skein; 94 yds (86 m)

Main Color (MC)
1 skein: shade Green Peka K04

Contrast Color 1 (CC1)
1 skein: shade Blue Awa K15

Contrast Color 2 (CC2)
1 skein: shade Ashen K13

NEEDLES:

US 7 (4.5 mm) straight and set of double-pointed needles

GAUGE:

US 7 (4.5 mm) needles, 15 stitches x 22 rows = 4 in (10 cm) over stocking stitch. Adjust the needle size as needed to get the correct tension.

Using MC, cast on 11 (21) stitches using US 7 (4.5 mm) straight needles:

Row 1: *k1tbl, p1*, repeat from *to* to the last stitch, k1tbl, turn, cast on 5 stitches (16, 26 stitches).

Row 2: *k1, p1tbl*, repeat from *to* to the end of the row, turn, cast on 5 stitches (21, 31 stitches).

Row 3: *p1, k1tbl*, repeat from *to* to the last stitch, k1tbl, turn, cast on 5 stitches (26, 36 stitches).

Row 4: *p1tbl, k1*, repeat from *to* to the end of the row, turn, cast on 5 stitches (31, 41 stitches).

Row 5: *k1tbl, p1*, repeat from *to* to the last stitch, k1tbl, turn, cast on 5 stitches (36, 46 stitches).

Row 6: *k1, p1tbl*, repeat from *to* to the end of the row, turn, cast on 5 stitches (41, 51 stitches).

Row 7: *p1, k1tbl*, repeat from *to* to the last stitch, p1, turn, cast on 5 stitches (46, 56 stitches).

Row 8: *p1tbl, k1*, repeat from *to* to the end of the row, turn, cast on 5 stitches (51, 61 stitches).

Row 9: *k1tbl, p1*, repeat from *to* to the last stitch, k1tbl, turn, cast on 5 stitches (56, 66 stitches).

Row 10: *k1, p1tbl*, repeat from *to* to the end of the row,, turn, cast on 5 stitches (61, 71 stitches).

Row 11: *p1, k1tbl*, repeat from *to* to the last stitch, p1, turn, cast on 5 stitches (66, 76 stitches).

Row 12: *p1tbl, k1*, repeat from *to* to the end of the row, turn, cast on 5 stitches (71, 81 stitches).

Row 13: *k1tbl, p1*, repeat from *to* to the last stitch, k1tbl, turn, cast on 5 stitches (76, 86 stitches).

Row 14: *k1, p1tbl*, repeat from *to* to the end of the row, turn, cast on 5 stitches (81, 91 stitches).

Row 15: *p1, k1tbl*, repeat from *to* to the last stitch, p1, turn, cast on 9 stitches (90, 100 stitches).

Spread these stitches evenly over 3 of the double-pointed needles.

Place marker, if using, and slip on every round. Start to work in the round — do not turn the needles at the end of the round, just keep going in the same direction, working with the right side facing.

Work 8 rounds of p1, k1tbl, rib without any increasing.

Break off MC.

Join in CC1 to the bottom edge of the ribbed section:

Round 1 (CC1): knit.

Round 2 (CC1): loosely bind off knitwise.

For the main part of the hat, with the right side facing, pick up 90 (100) stitches evenly around the cast-on edge of the ribbed band with CC1 and spread evenly over 3 double-pointed needles:

Place marker, if using, and slip on every round.

Round 1 (CC1): knit.

Round 2 (CC1) (increase): *kfb, p1*, repeat from *to* to the end of the round (135, 150 stitches).

Round 3 (CC1): *k2, p1*, repeat from *to* to the end of the round.

Round 4 (CC1) (decrease): *sl1, k1, psso, p1*, repeat from *to* to the end of the round (90, 100 stitches).

Round 5 (CC1): knit.

Round 6 (CC1) (decrease): *sl1, k1, psso, k7 (8)*, repeat from *to* to the end of the round (80, 90 stitches).

Join in CC2:

Round 7 (CC2): knit.

Round 8 (CC2): purl.

Rejoin in MC:

Round 9 (MC) (decrease): *sl1, k1, psso, k6 (7)*, repeat from *to* to the end of the round (70, 80 stitches).

Round 10 (MC): purl.

Rejoin in CC1:

Round 11 (CC1) (decrease):*sl1, k1, psso, k5 (6)*, repeat from *to* to the end of the round (60, 70 stitches).

Round 12 (CC1) (increase): *kfb, p1*, repeat from *to* to the end of the round (90, 105 stitches).

Round 13 (CC1): *k2, p1*, repeat from *to* to the end of the round.

Round 14 (CC1) (decrease): *sl1, k1, psso, p1*, repeat from *to* to the end of the round (60, 70 stitches).

Round 15 (CC1): knit.

Round 16 (CC1) (decrease): *sl1, k1, psso, k4 (5)*, repeat from *to* to the end of the round (50, 60 stitches).

Rejoin in CC2, but do not break off CC1:

Round 17: *k1 CC1, k1 CC2*, repeat from *to* to the end of the round.

Rounds 18–20 (CC2): knit.

Rejoin in MC, but do not break off CC2:

Round 21: *k1 CC2, k1 MC*, repeat from *to* to the end of the round.

Rounds 22 & 23 (MC): knit.

Round 24 (MC) (decrease): *sl1, k1, psso, k3 (4)*, repeat from *to* to the end of the round (40, 50 stitches).

Rejoin in CC2:

Round 25 (CC2): knit.

Round 26 (CC2): purl.

Rejoin in CC1:

Round 27 (CC1) (decrease): *sl1, k1, psso,

k2 (3)*, repeat from *to* to the end of the round (30, 40 stitches).

Round 28 (CC1): purl.

Rejoin in MC:

Round 29 (MC): knit.

Round 30 (MC) (decrease): *sl1, k1, psso, k1 (2)*, repeat from *to* to the end of the round (20, 30 stitches).

Rejoin in CC2, but do not break off MC:

Round 31: *k1 CC2, k1 MC*, repeat from *to* to the end of the round. Break off MC.

Round 32 (CC2) (decrease): *sl1, k1, psso, k0 (1)* repeat from *to* to the end of the round (10, 20 stitches).

Round 33 (CC2) (decrease): *sl1, k1, psso* repeat from *to* to the end of the round (5, 10 stitches).

Stop here for small–medium size.

Round 34 (CC2) (decrease): *sl1, k1, psso*, repeat from *to* to the end of the round (5 stitches).

Draw tail through remaining stitches and pull tight. Feed through to wrong side and tie off.

TO FINISH

Break off yarn leaving an 8 in (20 cm) tail and tie off securely. Using a darning needle, sew through the center a few times, ensuring no gaps remain. Weave yarn tails into stitches on the wrong side.

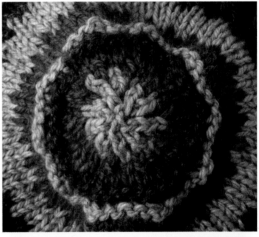

SLOUCH VEST

Knitted in the round | Level: Easy–Intermediate

When I started designing this, I was aiming for a vest you could throw over almost anything. At the same time, I was determined to add some color: so many of our clothes seem to be monotone, or dark colors, these days. It's a simple pattern that is worked from the collar down with raglan inserts for the shoulders, ending with the bottom row of the rib. There are no side seams and the main body is worked in the round. You could make this with any number of colors, or just a single contrasting color.

FINISHED MEASUREMENTS:

Small: chest 57 in (144.75 cm) and length 24 in (60 cm)

Medium: chest 58½ in (148.5 cm) and length 26 in (66 cm)

Large: chest 60 in (152.5 cm) and length 27½ in (70 cm)

YARN:

Rare Yarns Rotoiti Alpaca Merino 10 ply

80% alpaca, 20% merino; 1.75 oz (50 g) skein; 97 yds (88.5 m)

Main Color (MC) 5 (6, 6) skeins: shade Charming In Charcoal #509

Contrast Color 1 (CC1) 4 skeins: shade Green With Envy #507

Contrast Color 2 (CC2) 4 skeins: shade Tattoo Me Topaz #506

NEEDLES:

US 7 (4.5 mm) 16 in (40 cm) and 24 in (60 cm) circular needles, plus US 4 (3.5 mm) 16 in (40 cm) and 24 in (60 cm) circular needles

GAUGE:

Using US 7 (4.5 mm) needles, 16 stitches x 23 rows = 4 in (10 cm) over stocking stitch. Adjust the needle size to get the correct tension.

To start the collar, using MC, cast on 80 (100, 120) stitches with US 7 (4.5 mm) 16 in (40 cm) circular needle:

Keep knitting around the circle, with the right side of your work facing you, until your work measures 4 in (10 cm) from the cast-on edge.

Start the raglan inserts:

You may find it helps to place a marker at the beginning of the round and even before and after the increase sections, if you have enough (to do this, you will need 8 in total). Slip the marker on every round following.

Round 1 (MC) (increase): yo, k10 (14, 18), yo, k2, yo, k26 (32, 38), yo, k2, yo, k10 (14, 18), yo, k2, yo, k26 (32, 38), yo, k2 (88, 108, 128 stitches).

Round 2 (MC) (increase): yo, k12 (16, 20), yo, k2, yo, k28 (34, 40), yo, k2, yo, k12 (16, 20), yo, k2, yo, k28 (34, 36), yo, k2 (96, 116, 136 stitches).

Change to US 7 (4.5 mm) 24 in (60 cm) circular needle and start to add in contrast colors. Join in CC1:

Round 3 (CC1) (increase): yo, k14 (18, 22), yo, k2, yo, k30 (36, 42), yo, k2, yo, k14 (18, 22), yo, k2, yo, k30 (36, 42), yo, k2 (104, 124, 144 stitches).

Round 4 (CC1) (increase): yo, k16 (20, 24), yo, k2, yo, k32 (38, 44), yo, k2, yo, k16 (20, 24), yo, k2, yo, k32 (38, 44), yo, k2 (112, 132, 152 stitches).

Change to MC:

Round 5 (MC) (increase): yo, k18 (22, 26), yo, k2, yo, k34 (40, 46), yo, k2, yo, k18 (22, 26), yo, k2, yo, k34 (40, 46), yo, k2 (120, 140, 160 stitches).

Round 6 (MC) (increase): yo, k20 (24, 28), yo, k2, yo, k36 (42, 48), yo, k2, yo, k20 (24, 28), yo, k2, yo, k36 (42, 48), yo, k2 (128, 148, 168 stitches).

Change to CC2:

Round 7 (CC2) (increase): yo, k22 (26, 30), yo, k2, yo, k38 (44, 50), yo, k2, yo, k22 (26, 30), yo, k2, yo, k38 (44, 50), yo, k2 (136, 156, 176 stitches).

Round 8 (CC2) (increase): yo, k24 (28, 32), yo, k2, yo, k40 (46, 52), yo, k2, yo, k24 (28, 32), yo, k2, yo, k40 (46, 52), yo, k2 (144, 164, 184 stitches).

Change to MC:

Round 9 (MC) (increase): yo, k26 (30, 34), yo, k2, yo, k42 (48, 54), yo, k2, yo, k26 (30, 34), yo, k2, yo, k42 (48, 54), yo, k2 (152, 172, 192 stitches).

Round 10 (MC) (increase): yo, k28 (32, 36), yo, k2, yo, k44 (50, 56), yo, k2, yo, k28 (32, 36), yo, k2, yo, k44 (50, 56), yo, k2 (160, 180, 200 stitches).

Change to CC1:

Round 11 (CC1) (increase): yo, k30 (34, 38), yo, k2, yo, k46 (52, 58), yo, k2, yo, k30 (34, 38), yo, k2, yo, k46 (52, 58), yo, k2 (168, 188, 208 stitches).

Round 12 (CC1) (increase): yo, k32 (36, 40), yo, k2, yo, k48 (54, 60), yo, k2, yo, k32 (36, 40), yo, k2, yo, k48 (54, 60), yo, k2 (176, 196, 216 stitches).

Change to MC:

Round 13 (MC) (increase): yo, k34 (38, 42), yo, k2, yo, k50 (56, 62), yo, k2, yo, k34 (38, 42), yo, k2, yo, k50 (56, 62), yo, k2 (184, 204, 224 stitches).

Round 14 (MC) (increase): yo, k36 (40, 44), yo, k2, yo, k52 (58, 64), yo, k2, yo, k36 (40, 44), yo, k2, yo, k52 (58, 64), yo, k2 (192, 212, 232 stitches).

Change to CC2:

Round 15 (CC2) (increase): yo, k38 (42, 46), yo, k2, yo, k54 (60, 66), yo, k2, yo, k38 (42, 46), yo, k2, yo, k54 (60, 66), yo, k2 (200, 220, 240 stitches).

Round 16 (CC2) (increase): yo, k40 (44, 48), yo, k2, yo, k56 (62, 68), yo, k2, yo, k40 (44, 48), yo, k2, yo, k56 (62, 68), yo, k2 (208, 228, 248 stitches).

Change to MC:

Round 17 (MC) (increase): yo, k42 (46, 50), yo, k2, yo, k58 (64, 70), yo, k2, yo, k42 (46, 50), yo, k2, yo, k58 (64, 70), yo, k2 (216, 236, 256 stitches).

Round 18 (MC) (increase): yo, k44 (48, 52), yo, k2, yo, k60 (66, 72), yo, k2, yo, k44 (48, 52), yo, k2, yo, k60 (66, 72), yo, k2 (224, 244, 264 stitches).

Change to CC1:

Round 19 (CC1) (increase): yo, k46 (50, 54), yo, k2, yo, k62 (68, 74), yo, k2, yo, k46 (50, 54), yo, k2, yo, k62 (68, 74), yo, k2 (232, 252, 272 stitches).

Round 20 (CC1) (increase): yo, k48 (52, 56), yo, k2, yo, k64 (70, 76), yo, k2, yo, k48 (52, 56), yo, k2, yo, k64 (70, 76), yo, k2 (240, 260, 280 stitches).

Change to MC:

Round 21 (MC) (increase): yo, k50 (54, 58), yo, k2, yo, k66 (72, 78), yo, k2, yo, k50 (54, 58), yo, k2, yo, k66 (72, 78), yo, k2, yo. (248, 268, 288 stitches).

Round 22 (MC) (increase): yo, k52 (56, 60), yo, k2, yo, k68 (74, 80), yo, k2, yo, k52 (56, 60), yo, k2, yo, k68 (74, 80), yo, k2 (256, 276, 296 stitches).

Change to CC2:

Round 23 (CC2) (increase): yo, k54 (58, 62), yo, k2, yo, k70 (76, 82), yo, k2, yo, k54 (58, 62), yo, k2, yo, k70 (76, 82), yo, k2 (264, 284, 304 stitches).

Round 24 (CC2) (increase): yo, k56 (60, 64), yo, k2, yo, k72 (78, 84), yo, k2, yo, k56 (60, 64), yo, k2, yo, k72 (78, 84), yo, k2 (272, 292, 312 stitches).

Change to MC:

Round 25 (MC) (increase): yo, k58 (62, 66), yo, k2, yo, k74 (80, 86), yo, k2, yo, k58 (62, 66), yo, k2, yo, k74 (80, 86), yo, k2 (280, 300, 320 stitches).

Round 26 (MC) (increase): yo, k60 (64, 68), yo, k2, yo, k76 (82, 88), yo, k2, yo, k60 (64, 68), yo, k2, yo, k76 (82, 88), yo, k2 (288, 308, 328 stitches).

Change to CC1:

Round 27 (CC1) (increase): yo, k62 (66, 70), yo, k2, yo, k78 (84, 90), yo, k2, yo, k62 (66, 70), yo, k2, yo, k78 (84, 90), yo, k2 (296, 316, 336 stitches).

Round 28 (CC1) (increase): yo, k64 (68, 72), yo, k2, yo, k80 (86, 92), yo, k2, yo, k64 (68, 72), yo, k2, yo, k80 (86, 92), yo, k2 (304, 324, 344 stitches).

Change to MC:

Round 29 (MC) (increase): yo, k66 (70, 74), yo, k2, yo, k82 (88, 94), yo, k2, yo, k66 (70, 74), yo, k2, yo, k82 (88, 94), yo, k2 (312, 332, 352 stitches).

Round 30 (MC) (increase): yo, k68 (72, 76), yo, k2, yo, k84 (90, 96), yo, k2, yo, k68 (72, 76), yo, k2, yo, k84 (90, 96), yo, k2 (320, 340, 360 stitches).

Change to CC2:

Round 31 (CC2) (increase): yo, k70 (74, 78), yo, k2, yo, k86 (92, 98), yo, k2, yo, k70 (74, 78), yo, k2,

yo, k86 (92, 98), yo, k2 (328, 348, 368 stitches).
Round 32 (CC2) (increase): yo, k72 (76, 80), yo, k2, yo, k88 (94, 100), yo, k2, yo, k72 (76, 80), yo, k2, yo, k88 (94, 100), yo, k2 (336, 356, 376 stitches).

Change to MC and stop increasing:

Round 33 (MC): k74 (78, 82), k2, k90 (96, 102), k2, k74 (78, 82), k2, k90 (96, 102), k2.

Bind off for shoulder edge:

Round 34 (MC): Bind off knitwise 74 (78, 82) stitches, k94 (100, 106), bind off knitwise 74 (78, 82) stitches, knit to the end of the round.

You should have 2 groups of 94 (100, 106) stitches which are for the front and back sections.

Start working the main body:

You will be working the front and back separately for the next 18 rows (or 6 if small size) as if on straight needles. You can still use the circular needle and do both at the same time, but will need to join an extra skein of yarn to do that. The width of the contrast rows will be increasing, but with just 2 rows of MC in between.

Row 1 (CC1): knit.
Row 2 (CC1): purl.
Row 3 (CC1): knit.
Row 4 (CC1): purl.
Row 5 (MC): knit.
Row 6 (MC): purl.

Stop here for small size and continue with next 12 rows for medium and large sizes:

Row 7 (CC2): knit.
Row 8 (CC2): purl.
Repeat rows 7 & 8.
Repeat rows 5-6.
Repeat rows 1-6.

Start working in the round again to complete the main body, place marker, if using, and slip on every round (188, 200, 212 stitches):

Work 4 knit rounds in CC2.
Work 2 knit rounds in MC.
Work 4 knit rounds in CC1.
Work 2 knit rounds in MC.
Work 4 knit rounds in CC2.
Work 2 knit rounds in MC.
Work 8 knit rounds in CC1.
Work 2 knit rounds in MC.
Work 8 knit rounds in CC2.
Work 2 knit rounds in MC.
Work 8 knit rounds in CC1.
Work 2 knit rounds in MC.
Stop here for small and medium sizes.
Work 8 knit rounds in CC2, for large size only.

Change to US 4 (3.5 mm) 24 in (60 cm) circular needle to complete rib, for all sizes:

Rib round: *k1tbl, p1*, repeat from *to* to the end of the round.

Repeat this round until rib measures 3 in (7.5 cm).

Bind off knitwise.

To complete armholes, using MC pick up and knit 102 (116, 120) stitches with US 4 (3.5 mm) 6 in (15 cm) circular needle around each armhole:

Rib round: *k1tbl, p1*, repeat from *to* to the end of the round.

Repeat this round until rib measures 1 in (2.5 cm).

Bind off knitwise.

TO FINISH

Break off yarn leaving an 8 in (20 cm) tail and tie off securely. Using a darning needle, weave yarn tails into stitches on the wrong side. The collar should roll over naturally, but if it doesn't, roll it so the wrong side is visible.

SOU'WESTER HAT

Knitted flat and in the round   Level: Intermediate–Advanced

FINISHED MEASUREMENTS:

This hat will fit head circumference from 20–23 in (50.75–58.5 cm)

YARN:

Zealana Artisan Series Heron/worsted weight

80% fine merino, 20% brushtail possum yarn; 1.76 oz (50 g) skein; 109 yds (100 m)

2 skeins: shade H12 Honey

NEEDLES:

US 8 (5 mm) double-pointed needles plus cable needle

GAUGE:

Using US 8 (5 mm) needles, 16 stitches x 24 rows = 4 in (10 cm) over k2, p2 pattern *before felting*. Adjust the needle size as needed to get the correct tension.

The overlapping series of cable stitches in this hat creates a woven appearance. It has a two-by-two rib brim that is deliberately loose so it can be folded over or pulled down low against the weather. The pattern looks complicated but once you get started, it gets easier as it is repeated throughout the whole hat. I used a merino/possum blend which has a slight tweed look. I felted the hat lightly once completed. It would look good in any plain or 'tweedy' yarn but possibly not a highly variegated one. This is a pattern where a round marker would be useful.

Using US 8 (5 mm) double-pointed needles, cast on 128 stitches and divide them evenly across three needles:

Round 1: *p2, k2*, repeat from *to* to the end of the round.

Repeat round 1 until work measures 2¾ in (7 cm).

Start cable pattern:

Place marker, if using, and slip on every round.

Round 2 (cable round): *sl2 onto cn, hold at front, k2, p2, k2 from the cn, p2*, repeat from *to* to the end of the round.

Rounds 3–5: *k2, p2*, repeat from *to* to the end of the round.

Round 6 (cable round): k2, p2, *sl2 onto cn, hold at back, k2, p2, k2 from the cn, p2*, repeat from *to* to last 4 stitches before the marker, *sl2 onto cn, hold at back, p2, slip marker, k2 from left-hand needle (these last 2 stitches are the same stitches you worked at the start of this round), place marker, k2 from the cn.

Rounds 7–9: *p2, k2*, repeat from *to* to the end of the round.

Note: In order to keep the basket weave appearance, on the cable rounds you will be incorporating stitches from the next round. I find it easier not to use a marker and just follow the pattern, but a marker may help while you establish the pattern.

Repeat rounds 2–9 until your work measures 7 in (17.75 cm) from the cast-on edge, ending with round 9.

Start decreasing for the crown:

Round 1 (cable round) (decrease): *sl2 onto cn, hold at front, k2, p2tog, k2 from the cn, p2*, repeat from *to* to the end of the round (112 stitches).

Round 2: *k2, p1, k2, p2*, repeat from *to* to the end of the round.

Round 3 (decrease): *k2, p1, k2, p2tog*, repeat from *to* to the end of round, place marker (96 stitches).

Round 4: *k2, p1, k2, p1*, repeat from *to* to the end of the round.

Round 5 (cable round) (decrease): k2, p1, *sl2 onto cn, hold at back, k2tog, p1, k2 from the cn, p1*, repeat from *to* to last 3 stitches before the marker, sl2 onto cn, hold at back, k2tog, p1 from left-hand needle, place marker, k2 from the cn (80 stitches).

Round 6: *k1, p1, k2, p1*, repeat from *to* to the end of the round.

Round 7 (decrease): *k1, p1, k2tog, p1*, repeat from *to* to the end of the round (64 stitches).

Round 8: *k1, p1*, repeat from *to* to the end of the round.

Round 9 (decrease): *sl1, k2tog, psso, p1*, repeat from *to* to the end of the round (32 stitches).

Round 10: *k1, p1*, repeat from *to* to the end of the round.

Round 11 (decrease): k2tog, repeat to the end of the round (16 stitches).

Round 12 (decrease): k2tog, repeat to the end of the round (8 stitches).

TO FINISH

Break off yarn leaving an 8 in (20 cm) tail and draw tail through remaining stitches. Pull tight and feed through to wrong side and tie off. Using a darning needle, sew through the center a few times, ensuring no gaps remain. Wash the hat in warm soapy water (use a wool wash detergent) and agitate until the fibers start to felt. Be careful not to overdo it. When it is about 10% smaller, rinse thoroughly with warm water and lay the hat flat to dry.

UP THE MOUNTAIN

BRACED FOR THE ELEMENTS

WOMAN'S SHAPED VEST

Knitted in the round   Level: Advanced

This is by far the softest yarn in the book and the finished vest feels absolutely wonderful. It is both lightweight and beautifully textured. The collar, which is inset into the deep V of the front, is worked in a single piece at the end. This yarn is a little thicker than a standard DK yarn, so keep that in mind if substituting with another yarn.

FINISHED MEASUREMENTS:

Small: bust 33–35 in (83.75–89 cm)

Medium: bust 36–38 in (91.5–96.5 cm)

Large: bust 39–41 in (99–104 cm)

YARN:

Lion Brand LB Collection Angora Merino DK

80% extrafine merino; 20% angora; 1.76 oz (50 g) skein; 131 yds (120 m)

5 (5, 6) skeins: shade #491 Parchment

NEEDLES:

US 8 (5 mm) 16–20 in (40–60 cm) circular needle and a US 7 (4.5 mm) 16–20 in (40–60 cm) circular needle, or US 7 (4.5 mm) double-pointed needles

GAUGE:

Using US 8 (5 mm) needles, 22 stitches x 18 rows = 4 in (10 cm) over stocking stitch. Adjust the needle size as needed to get the correct tension.

To start, cast on 152 (160, 168) stitches with US 8 (5 mm) circular needle:

Work in the round, place marker, if using, and slip on every round. Do not turn the needles at the end of the round, just keep going in the same direction, working on the right side of work.

Round 1: knit.

Round 2: *k1tbl, p1*, repeat from *to* to the end of the round.

Repeat round 2 until work measures 6 in (15.25 cm).

Divide at the front and start working in rows:

For the remainder of the body, you will be using the circular needle as if it is 2 straight needles, which means you will turn at the end of each row. Every second row, there is a decrease at the neck edge.

Foundation row: slip first stitch onto a holder (to be used for the collar later), working on remaining stitches only, *p1, k1tbl* repeat from *to* to the last stitch, p1, turn (151, 159, 167 stitches).

Row 1: (k1, p1tbl) 4 times, purl to last 8 stitches, (p1tbl, k1) 4 times.

Row 2 (decrease): (p1, k1tbl) 3 times, sl1, k1, psso, knit to the last 8 stitches, k2tog, (p1tbl, k1) 3 times, p1tbl (149, 157, 165 stitches).

Repeat rows 1 & 2, 14 times and your work measures 13 in (33 cm) from the cast-on edge (121, 129, 137 stitches). If short, repeat row 1 without shaping to reach the required length.

Divide for the armhole:

Row 1 (decrease): (p1, k1tbl) 3 times, p1, sl1, k1, psso, k15 (16, 18), bind off 2 (3, 4) stitches knitwise, k68 (72, 74), bind off 2 (3, 4) stitches, k14 (15, 17), k2tog, (p1, k1tbl) 3 times, p1 (115, 121, 127 stitches).

You should have three groups of stitches — 23 (24, 26) for each of the two fronts and 69 (73, 75), for the back. Instructions are provided to complete each front and back separately. Keep working on the circular needle as if it was 2 straight needles, turning at the end of each row.

Begin working on the left-hand front, with wrong side facing (23, 24, 26 stitches):

Continue decreasing at neck edge every second row and at the same time decrease at armhole every row for the next 4 rows.

LH row 1 (decrease): (k1, p1tbl) 4 times, p13 (14, 16), p2tog (22, 23, 25 stitches).

LH row 2 (decrease): sl1, k1, psso, k11 (12, 14), k2tog, p1, (k1tbl, p1) 3 times (20, 21, 23 stitches).

LH row 3 (decrease): (k1, p1tbl) 4 times, p10 (11, 13), p2tog (19, 20, 22 stitches).

Row 4 (decrease): sl1, k1, psso, k8 (9, 11), k2tog, p1, (k1tbl, p1) 3 times (17, 18, 20 stitches).

Stop decreasing at neck edge for all sizes, but continue decreasing at armhole edge for medium and large sizes.

For medium size only (18 stitches):

LH row 5 (decrease): (k1, p1tbl) 4 times, p8, p2tog (17 stitches).

LH row 6: k9, (k1tbl, p1) 4 times.

For large size only (20 stitches):

LH row 5 (decrease): (k1, p1tbl) 4 times, p10, p2tog (19 stitches).

LH row 6 (decrease): sl1, k1, psso, k9, (k1tbl, p1) 4 times (18 stitches).

LH row 7 (decrease): (k1, p1tbl) 4 times, p8, p2tog (17 stitches).

LH row 8: k9, (k1tbl, p1) 4 times.

All sizes now have 17 stitches. Keeping pattern correct, continue working on these 17 stitches. Decrease at armhole edge on the fourth row (16 stitches), then continue straight until work measures 23 in (58.5 cm) from cast-on edge. Do not bind off, move stitches onto a holder.

Rejoin yarn at the armhole edge of the right-hand front with wrong side facing (23, 24, 26 stitches):

Continue decreasing at neck edge every second row and at the same time decrease at armhole every row for the next 4 rows.

RH row 1 (decrease): sl1, p1, psso, p13 (14, 16), (p1tbl, k1) 4 times (22, 23, 25 stitches).

RH row 2 (decrease): (p1, k1tbl) 3 times, p1, sl1, k1, psso, k11 (12, 14), k2tog (20, 21, 23 stitches).

RH row 3 (decrease): sl1, p1, psso, p10 (11, 13), (p1tbl, k1) 4 times (19, 20, 22 stitches).

RH row 4 (decrease): (p1, k1tbl) 3 times, p1, sl1, k1, psso, k8 (9, 11), k2tog (17, 18, 20 stitches).

Stop decreasing at neck edge for all sizes, but continue decreasing at armhole edge for medium and large sizes.

For medium size only (18 stitches):

RH row 5 (decrease): sl1, p1, psso, p8, (p1tbl, k1) 4 times (17 stitches).

RH row 6: (p1, k1tbl) 4 times, k8.

For the large size only (20 stitches):

RH row 5 (decrease): sl1, p1, psso, p10, (p1tbl, k1) 4 times (19 stitches).

RH row 6 (decrease): (p1 k1tbl) 4 times, k10, k2tog (18 stitches).

RH row 7 (decrease): sl1, p1, psso, p8, (k1, p1tbl) 4 times (17 stitches).

RH row 8: (p1 k1tbl) 4 times, k9.

All sizes now have 17 stitches. Keeping pattern correct, continue working on these 17 stitches. Decrease at armhole edge on the fourth row (16 stitches), then continue straight until work measures 23 in (58.5 cm) from cast-on edge. Do not bind off, move stitches onto a holder.

Rejoin yarn at the left-hand armhole edge of back with wrong side facing (69, 73, 75 stitches):

Decrease at armhole edges every row for the next 3 rows.

Row 1 (decrease): sl1, k1, psso, k65 (69, 71), k2tog (67, 71, 73 stitches).

Row 2 (decrease): sl1, p1, psso, p63 (67, 69), p2tog (65, 69, 71 stitches).

Row 3 (decrease): sl1, k1, psso, k61 (65, 67) k2tog (63, 67, 69 stitches).

Decrease at armhole edge every fourth row.

Row 4: purl.

Row 5: knit.

Row 6: purl.

Row 7 (decrease): sl1, k1, psso, k59 (63, 65) k2tog (61, 65, 67 stitches).

Rows 8–10: repeat rows 4–6.

Row 11 (decrease): sl1, k1, psso, k57 (61, 63) k2tog (59, 63, 65 stitches)

Repeat rows 4 & 5 until work measures 23 in (58.5 cm) from cast-on edge.

Last row: k16, bind off 27 (31, 33) knitwise, k16.

To make shoulder seams:

With the right sides of the front and back together, hold the needles side by side and, using a third needle, pick up and knit 1 stitch together from each needle and, at the same time, loosely bind off all stitches knitwise to form the shoulder seam. If you prefer, you can bind off each separately and then sew them together, but I prefer this technique as it provides a lovely even seam.

To make the neck/collar, starting at the back and using a US 7 (4.5 mm) circular needle, pick up 161 (179, 189) stitches evenly around the neck edge:

When you get to the front, knit the stitch that you placed on a holder, as well as knitting into the loop either side of this stitch (162, 180, 190 stitches).

With the right side facing, work 3½ in (8.75 cm) of stocking stitch (just knit every round). At the same time, when you get to the front on the next and every round afterwards, stop 1 stitch before the middle 3 stitches and work as follows: k2tog, k1tbl, sl1, k1, psso.

Bind off.

To finish the armholes, with the right side facing and using US 7 (4.5 mm) circular needle, or US 7 (4.5 mm) double-pointed needles, pick up 86 (90, 98) stitches evenly around the armhole:

Rounds 1–4: (k1tbl, p1) repeat to the end of the round. Bind off loosely knitwise.

TO FINISH

Break off yarn leaving an 8 in (20 cm) tail and tie off securely. Using a darning needle, weave yarn tail into stitches on the wrong side.

SIMPLE STRIPED FINGERLESS GLOVES

Knitted in the round — Level: Easy

These striped fingerless gloves knit up quickly. I have chosen three strong colors and partnered them with the black shade of the same yarn for maximum contrast. They would look good in almost any color combination. I used a superwash merino from Lion Brand, which is closer to 5 ply in thickness so substituting another 8 ply yarn may make the sizes too big and you should check the gauge first. It comes in large skeins (3.5 oz/100 g) and I was able to make these gloves and a vest (page 61), hat (page 72) and mittens (page 69) from six skeins in total (one in each color).

FINISHED MEASUREMENTS:

Small: 8½ in (21.5 cm) long and 4 in (10 cm) wide

Medium: 9 in (22.75 cm) long and 4½ in (11.5 cm) wide

Large: 9½ in (24 cm) long and 5 in (12.75 cm) wide

YARN:

Lion Brand LB Collection Superwash Merino 8 ply

100% superwash merino; 3.5 oz (100 g) skein; 306 yds (280 m)

Contrast Color 1 (CC1) 1 skein: shade #170 Dijon

Contrast Color 2 (CC2) 1 skein: shade #153 Night Sky

Contrast Color 3 (CC3) 1 skein: shade #123 Hemp

Contrast Color 4 (CC4) 1 skein: shade #102 Aqua

Note: If using smaller skeins (1.76 oz/50 g) you will still only need one of each color, although not complete skeins. The total weight of this pair of gloves is 1.47 oz (42 g).

NEEDLES:

US 5 (3.75 mm) set of double-pointed needles

GAUGE:

Using US 5 (3.75 mm) needles, 20 stitches x 30 rows = 4 in (10 cm) over stripe pattern. Adjust the needle size to get the correct tension.

Both gloves use the same pattern, using CC1, cast on 34 (40, 46) stitches with US 5 (3.75 mm) double-pointed needles:

Distribute the stitches evenly across three of the needles and start working in the round. Place a marker, if using, and slip on every round.

Rounds 1–3 (CC1): *k1tbl, p1*, repeat from *to* to the end.

Round 4 (change to CC2): knit.

Rounds 5 & 6 (CC2): *k1tbl, p1*, repeat from *to* to the end.

Round 7 (change to CC3): knit.

Rounds 8 & 9 (CC3): *k1tbl, p1*, repeat from *to* to the end.

Round 10 (change to CC4): knit.

Rounds 11 & 12 (CC4): *k1tbl, p1*, repeat from *to* to the end.

Round 13: (CC1): knit.

Repeat rounds 2–13 until the rib measures approximately 3½ in (8.75 cm).

Stop rib pattern and start working in stocking stitch (knit all rounds), working the following color sequence:

Knit 1 round CC1.

Knit 1 round CC2.

Knit 1 round CC3.

Knit 1 round CC4.

Repeat this until work measures 5 in (12.75 cm) from the start.

Keeping the stripe pattern correct, start to increase for thumb:

Round 1 (increase): k17 (20, 23), kfb, k16 (19, 22), (35, 41, 47 stitches).

Round 2 (increase): k16 (19, 22), kfb, k2, kfb, k15 (18, 21), (37, 43, 49 stitches).

Round 3 (increase): k16 (19, 22), kfb, k4, kfb, k15 (18, 21), (39, 45, 51 stitches).

Round 4 (increase): k16 (19, 22), kfb, k6, kfb, k15 (18, 21), (41, 47, 53 stitches).

Round 5 (increase): k16 (19, 22), kfb, k8, kfb, k15 (18, 21), (43, 49, 55 stitches).

Keeping the stripe pattern correct, knit every row until work measures 6½ (7, 7½) in (16.5, 17.75, 19 cm) from cast-on edge.

Separate for thumb:

K16 (19, 21), knit next 11 (11, 13) stitches then place them onto stitch holder, k16 (19, 21).

Keep working in the round on these 32 (38, 42) stitches, keeping the stripe pattern correct, until your work measures 7½ (8, 8½) in (19, 20, 21.5 cm) from the cast-on edge.

Working in CC2 only, make the rib edge:

Round 1 (CC2): knit.

Rounds 2–6 (CC2): *k1tbl, p1*, repeat from *to* to the end.

Bind off loosely knitwise.

Rejoin CC2 to make the thumb rib edge and knit all of the 11 (11, 13) stitches placed on the holder:

Pick up and knit 3 (3, 3) stitches where the hand and thumb separate (14, 14, 16 stitches).

Rounds 1–3 (CC2): *k1tbl, p1*, repeat from *to* to the end.

Bind off knitwise.

Repeat for second glove.

TO FINISH

Break off yarn leaving an 8 in (20 cm) tail and tie off securely. Using a darning needle, weave yarn tails into stitches on the wrong side.

CLASSIC WEAVE SCARF

Knitted flat   Level: Intermediate

This lightweight scarf uses three different yarns and stitches in a way that creates a knitted fabric with a woven appearance. Every alternate row, the yarn is carried across the back of alternate slipped stitches. To get the woven tweed look, choose closely matched colors, which are worked in alternate rows. The scarf is knitted sideways: the longest edges are the cast-on and bind-off edges and each woven segment is divided by a raised knit row to create lengthwise wide stripes. This scarf is worked on a long circular needle to hold all of the stitches, but the pattern is worked in rows as if using straight needles. The fringe is created by leaving long (6 in/15 cm) yarn tails when you join each new color in.

FINISHED MEASUREMENTS:

The scarf is 57 in (144.75 cm) in length and 6 in (15.25 cm) wide. You can increase the length by adding extra stitches. For every 6 in (15 cm), add 28 stitches and you could add another stripe — each stripe equals approximately 6 in (15 cm).

YARN:

Patons Dreamtime 4 ply

100% merino; 1.76 oz (50 g) skein; 185 yds (169 m)

Naturally Waikiwi Prints 4 ply

55% merino, 20% nylon, 15% alpaca, 10% possum; 1.76 oz (50 g) skein; 198 yds (181 m)

Main Color (MC)
1 skein: Patons Dreamtime 4 ply, shade 2958 Charcoal

Contrast Color 1 (CC1)
1 skein: Patons Dreamtime 4 ply, shade 2957 Donkey

Contrast Color 2 (CC2)
1 skein: Naturally Waikiwi Prints, shade 464

NEEDLES:

US 3 (3.25 mm) circular needle, at least 24 in (60 cm) in length

... cont. next page

To start the scarf, use MC and cast on 337 stitches with US 3 (3.25 mm) circular needle.

Row 1 (MC): knit, turn.

Break off MC, leaving a 6 in (15 cm) tail. Join CC1, leaving a 6 in (15 cm) tail.

Row 2 (CC1): *p1, yb, sl1 purlwise and, at the same time, carry yarn across back of work, yf*, repeat from *to* to the last stitch, p1.

Break off CC1, leaving a 6 in (15 cm) tail and rejoin MC, leaving a 6 in (15 cm) tail.

Rows 3–10: repeat rows 1 & 2, 4 more times, switching between MC and CC1 for each row.

Break off CC1 leaving a 6 in (15 cm) tail and rejoin MC, leaving a 6 in (15 cm) tail.

Rows 11–12 (MC): knit.

Row 13 (MC): knit.

Break off MC, leaving a 6 in (15 cm) tail. Join CC2, leaving a 6 in (15 cm) tail.

Row 14 (CC2): *p1, yb, sl1 purlwise and, at the same time, carry yarn across back of work, yf*, repeat from *to* to the last stitch, p1.

GAUGE:

Using US 3 (3.25 mm) needles, 20 stitches x 40 rows = 4 in (10 cm). Adjust the needle size as needed to get the correct tension.

Break off CC2, leaving a 6 in (15 cm) tail. Rejoin MC, leaving a 6 in (15 cm) tail.

Rows 15–22: repeat rows 13 & 14, 4 more times.

Break off CC2 leaving a 6 in (15 cm) tail and rejoin MC, leaving a 6 in (15 cm) tail.

Rows 23–24 (MC): knit.

Rows 25–34: repeat rows 1–10.

Break off CC1 leaving a 6 in (15 cm) tail and rejoin MC, leaving a 6 in (15 cm) tail.

Rows 35–36 (MC): knit.

Rows 37–46: repeat rows 13–22.

Break off CC2 leaving a 6 in (15 cm) tail and rejoin MC, leaving a 6 in (15 cm) tail.

Rows 47–48 (MC): knit.

Rows 49–58: repeat rows 1–10.

Break off CC1 leaving a 6 in (15 cm) tail and rejoin MC, leaving a 6 in (15 cm) tail.

Row 59 (MC): knit.

Bind off loosely knitwise.

TO FINISH

Make sure ends of yarn are tied off and starting at one short edge, grasp two of the yarn tails and tie a knot firmly at the base. Continue until all yarn tails are secure. Repeat for the other end. Trim fringe to make it even.

REVERSIBLE MOSAIC HAT

Knitted in the round   Level: Intermediate–Advanced

This fully reversible hat is double-layered and incredibly warm. It feels soft and light to wear, mostly because it is worked in a 4 ply yarn that has some very airy fibers (alpaca and possum mixed with merino). There is also a touch of nylon in this mix, which provides some stretch.

I have used a variegated yarn and chosen a color in the same yarn for contrast, but you could use any 4 ply yarn. It would look just as effective in two plain colors.

FINISHED MEASUREMENTS:

Extra small: 19¼ in (48.75 cm) head circumference

Small: 20¼ in (51.5 cm) head circumference

Medium: 21¼ in (54 cm) head circumference

Large: 23¼ in (59 cm) head circumference

YARN:

Naturally Waikiwi 4 ply

55% merino, 20% nylon, 15% alpaca, 10% possum; 1.76 oz (50 g) skein; 198 yds (181 m)

Main Color (MC)
2 skeins: shade #464

Contrast Color (CC)
2 skeins: shade #419

NEEDLES:

US 3 (3.25 mm) set of double-pointed needles or 16 in (40 cm) circular needle

GAUGE:

Using US 3 (3.25 mm) needles, 24 stitches x 29 rows = 4 in (10 cm) over pattern. Adjust the needle size as needed to get the correct tension.

CHART SYMBOLS

/	k2tog
	knit MC
▓	knit CC

Using the main color (variegated), cast on 120 (126, 132, 144) stitches with US 3 (3.25 mm) double-pointed needles or circular needle:

Distribute the stitches evenly across three of the needles, if using double-pointed needles. Start working in the round. Do not turn your work, keep knitting around the circle, with the right side of your work facing you. Place marker, if using, and slip on every round.

Work 2 rounds knit in MC, then work 45 rounds of the pattern according to chart 1, starting at round 1. This pattern is worked over 6 stitches. Carry the other color yarn behind as you work, but be careful not to pull it too tight as you work across the round.

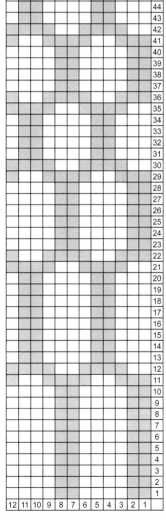

CHART 1

Start decreasing for crown:

Follow chart 2 (below) from round 46, decrease evenly across the round (k3 MC, k2tog CC). The pattern is now worked over 5 stitches (100, 105, 110, 120 stitches).

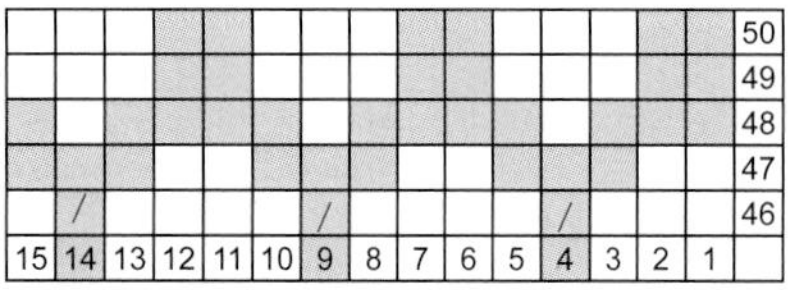

															50
															49
															48
															47
	/				/				/						46
15	14	13	12	11	10	9	8	7	6	5	4	3	2	1	

CHART 2

Work rows 47–50 as per chart 2 without decreasing.

Continue decreasing for crown:

Follow chart 3 (below) from round 51, decreasing evenly across the round (k2tog CC, k3 MC). The pattern is now worked over 4 stitches (80, 84, 88, 96 stitches).

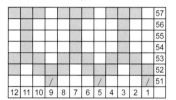

CHART 3

Work rows 52–57 as per chart 3 without decreasing.

Change to double-pointed needles if using a circular needle and continue decreasing further for the crown (not on chart):

Round 58 (decrease): *k1 MC, sl1, k2tog CC, psso*, repeat from *to* to the end of the round (40, 42, 44, 48) stitches).

Rounds 59 & 60: *k1 MC, k1 CC*, repeat from *to* to the end of the round.

Continue for extra small size (40 stitches):

Round 61 (decrease): *k1 MC, sl1, k2tog CC, psso*, repeat from *to* to the end of the round (20 stitches).

Round 62 (decrease): *k1 MC, sl1, k2tog CC, psso*, repeat from *to* to the end of the round (10 stitches).

Break off yarn, pull through the stitches on the needles and tie off securely.

Continue for small size (42 stitches):

Round 61 (decrease): *k1 MC, sl1, k2tog CC, psso, k1 MC, k1 CC*, repeat from *to* to the end of the round (28 stitches).

Round 62: *k1 MC, k1 CC*, repeat from *to* to the end of the round.

Round 63 (decrease): *k2tog MC, k2tog CC*, repeat from *to* to the end of the round (14 stitches).

Break off yarn, pull through the stitches on the needles and tie off securely.

Continue for medium size (44 stitches):

Round 61 (decrease): *k1 MC, sl1, k2tog CC, psso*, repeat from *to* to the end of the round (22 stitches).

Round 62: *k1 MC, k1 CC*, repeat from *to* to the end of the round.

Round 63 (decrease): *k2tog MC, k2tog CC*, repeat from *to* to the end of the round (11 stitches).

Break off yarn, pull through the stitches on the needles and tie off securely.

Continue for large size (48 stitches):

Round 61 (decrease): *k1 MC, sl1, k2tog CC, psso, k1 MC, k1 CC*, repeat from *to* to the end of the round (32 stitches).

Round 62: *k1 MC, k1 CC*, repeat from *to* to the end of the round.

Round 63 (decrease): *k2tog MC, k2tog CC*, repeat from *to* to the end of the round (16 stitches).

Round 64 (decrease): *k2tog MC, k2tog CC*, repeat from *to* to the end of the round (8 stitches).

Break off yarn, pull through the stitches on the needles and tie off securely.

Complete inside layer:

Using MC, with right-side facing, using US 3

(3.25 mm) double-pointed needles pick up and knit 120 (126, 132, 144) stitches along the cast-on edge. Place marker, if using, and slip on every round.

Work 1 round knit in MC.

Follow instructions above for the pattern, beginning round 1, but reverse the colors.

TO FINISH

Break off yarn leaving an 8 in (20 cm) tail and tie off securely. Using a darning needle, sew through the top of each layer to keep them together and to join the layers at the top of the hat. Weave yarn tails into stitches on the wrong side.

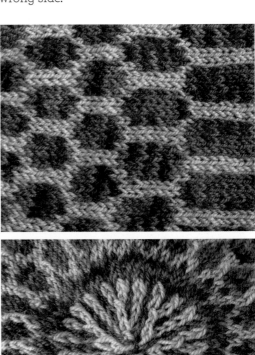

CABLED FINGERLESS GLOVES

Knitted in the round | Level: Intermediate

These fingerless gloves are made of a very fine 4 ply merino/possum/alpaca/nylon blend. The final effect is soft and warm and lightweight. The small percentage of nylon in this yarn adds some stretch and tension, which is accentuated by the ribbed pattern. They would also look great in a dark grey or brown color for a more rugged look.

FINISHED MEASUREMENTS:

Small: 8¾ in (22.25 cm) long and 3½ in (8.75 cm) wide

Medium: 10 in (25.5 cm) long and 4 in (10 cm) wide

Large: 11¼ in (28.5 cm) long and 4½ in (11.5 cm) wide

YARN:

Naturally Waikiwi 4 ply

55% merino, 20% nylon, 15% alpaca, 10% possum; 1.76 oz (50 g) skein; 198 yds (181 m)

1 skein: shade #419

NEEDLES:

US 2 (2.75 mm) set of double-pointed needles, plus a cable needle

GAUGE:

Using US 2 (2.75 mm) needles, 32 stitches x 36 rows = 4 in (10 cm) over k2, p2 rib pattern. Adjust the needle size as needed to get the correct tension.

To start the left-hand (LH) glove, cast on 54 (58, 62) stitches with US 2 (2.75 mm) double-pointed needles:

Distribute the stitches evenly across three of the needles and start working in the round. Place marker, if using, and slip on every round.

LH round 1: k2, p2, k20, *p2, k2*, repeat from *to* to the last 2 stitches, p2.

Repeat this round until work measures 3 in (7.5 cm) for all sizes.

Start cable pattern:

LH round 2 (cable): k2, p2, sl5 onto cn, hold cn at front, k5 from left-hand needle, k5 from cn, sl5 onto cn, hold cn at the back, k5 from left-hand needle, k5 from cn, *p2, k2*, repeat from *to* to the last 2 stitches, p2.

Repeat LH round 1, 8 (10, 12) more times.

Repeat LH round 2 (cable) once.

Make hole for thumb:

Stop working in rounds and, with the wrong side facing, work 6 (8, 10) rows, turning at the end of each row as if using straight needles.

LH row 1: *k2, p2*, repeat from *to* 6 (7, 8) more times, then k2, p20, p2, k2, turn.

LH row 2: k2, p2, k20, *p2, k2*, repeat from *to* to the last 2 stitches, p2, turn.

Repeat LH rows 1 & 2, 3 (4, 5) more times (8, 10, 12 rows in total).

LH row 3 (cable): k2, p2, sl5 onto cn, hold cn at front, k5 from

left-hand needle, k5 from cn, sl5 onto cn, hold cn at the back, k5 from left-hand needle, k5 from cn, *p2, k2*, repeat from *to* to the last 2 stitches, p2, turn.

Repeat LH rows 1 & 2, 4 (5, 6) times.

Repeat LH row 3 (cable) once. Do not turn work.

Start working in the round to join up again:

Place marker, if using, and slip on every round.

Repeat LH round 1, 8 (10, 12) more times.

Repeat LH round 2 (cable) once.

Repeat LH round 1, 8 (10, 12) more times.

Bind off loosely knitwise.

To start the RH glove cast on 54 (58, 62) stitches with US 2 (2.75 mm) double-pointed needles:

Distribute the stitches evenly across three of the needles and start working in the round. Place marker, if using, and slip on every round.

RH round 1: p2, *k2, p2*, repeat from *to* 6 (7, 8) times, k20, p2, k2.

Repeat this round until work measures 3 in (7.5 cm) for all sizes.

Start cable pattern:

RH round 2 (cable): p2, *k2, p2*, repeat from *to* 6 (7, 8) times, sl5 onto cn, hold cn at front, k5 from left-hand needle, k5 from cn, sl5 onto cn, hold cn at the back, k5 from left-hand needle, k5 from cn, p2, k2.

Repeat RH round 1, 8 (10, 12) more times.

Repeat RH round 2 (cable), once.

Make hole for thumb:

Stop working in rounds and, with the wrong side facing, work 6 (8, 10) rows, turning at the end of each row as if using straight needles.

RH row 1: k2, p2, k2, p20, *k2, p2*, repeat from *to* to the end, turn.

RH row 2: p2, *k2, p2*, repeat from *to* 6 (7, 8) times, k20, p2, k2, turn.

Repeat RH rows 1 & 2, 3 (4, 5) more times (8, 10, 12 rows in total).

RH row 3 (cable): p2, k2, p2, sl5 onto cn, hold cn at front, k5 from left-hand needle, k5 from cn, sl5 onto cn, hold cn at the back, k5 from left-hand needle, k5 from the cn, *p2, k2*, repeat from *to* to the end, turn.

Repeat RH rows 1 and 2, 4 (5, 6) times.

Repeat RH row 3 (cable), once. Do not turn work.

Start working in the round to join up again:

Repeat RH round 1, 8 (10, 12) more times.

Repeat RH round 2 (cable) once.

Repeat RH round 1, 8 (10, 12) more times.

Bind off loosely knitwise.

Finish thumbs:

Both thumbs are completed the same way. With right side facing and US 2 (2.75 mm) double-pointed needles, pick up and knit 32 (36, 40) stitches around the opening. Place row marker at beginning of round if you wish and slip on every round.

Thumb rounds 1–8: *k2, p2*, repeat from *to* to the end of the round.

Thumb round 9 (decrease): *k2, p2tog*, repeat from *to* to the end of the round (24, 27, 30 stitches).

Thumb round 10 (decrease): *k2tog, p1*, repeat from *to* to the end of the round (16, 18, 20 stitches).

Bind off loosely knitwise.

TO FINISH

Break off yarn leaving an 8 in (20 cm) tail and tie off securely. Using a darning needle, weave yarn tail into stitches on the wrong side.

BY THE LAKE

FRESH AIR FLAIR

CATCH A STAR VEST

Knitted in the round   Level: Intermediate–Advanced

When I started designing this vest, I was aiming for the 'wow' factor. I wanted to make something that made the wearer feel a little special no matter what they were doing. The colors and chevron pattern give it a vintage feel. Although you could use any number of colors, I think, for impact, you wouldn't want to use too few, but it could look stunning in two highly contrasting colors. I used a superwash merino from Lion Brand, which is closer to a 5 ply in thickness so substituting another 8 ply yarn may make the sizes too big and you should check the gauge first. It comes in large skeins (3.5 oz/100 g), and I was able to make this vest and a hat (page 72), fingerless gloves (page 45) and mittens (page 69) from six skeins in total (one in each color).

FINISHED MEASUREMENTS:

Small: bust 32–34 in (81.25–86.25 cm)

Medium: bust 35–38 in (89–96.5 cm)

Large: bust 39–41 in (99–104 cm)

YARN:

Lion Brand LB Collection Superwash Merino 8 ply

100% superwash merino; 3.5 oz (100 g) skein; 306 yds (280 m)

Main Color (MC) 1 skein: Ivory #098

Contrast Color 1 (CC1) 1 skein: #170 Dijon

Contrast Color 2 (CC2) 1 skein: #113 Cherry

Contrast Color 3 (CC3) 1 skein: #102 Aqua

Contrast Color 4 (CC4) 1 skein: #153 Night Sky

Contrast Color 5 (CC5) 1 skein: #123 Hemp

For larger sizes, you will need one extra skein of MC Ivory, or you could substitute another color in the body section.

... cont. next page

To start the collar, using MC (ivory), cast on 80 stitches with US 6 (4 mm) double-pointed needles or 14 in (35.5 cm) circular needle:

Distribute the stitches evenly across three of the needles and start working in the round. Do not turn your work; keep knitting around the circle, with the right side of your work facing you.

Using MC, work k2, p2 rib until your work measures 5 in (12.75 cm) from the cast-on edge.

Change to US 6 (4 mm) 14 in (35.5 cm) circular needle (if using double-pointed needles) and begin collar pattern. You may find it helps to place a marker and slip it at the end of each round:

Round 1 (MC) (increase): *k1, kfb, k3, k1, kfb, k2*, repeat from *to* to the end of the round (100 stitches).

Round 2 (MC): *yo, k3, sl1, k2tog, psso, k3, yo, k1*, repeat from *to* to the end of the round.

Round 3 (MC) (increase): *yo, k9, yo, k1*, repeat from *to* to the end of the round (120 stitches).

Round 4 (MC): *yo, k4, sl1, k2tog, psso, k4, yo, k1*, repeat from *to* to the end of the round.

NEEDLES:

US 6 (4 mm) set of double-pointed needles and US 6 (4 mm) 16 in (40 cm) and 24 in (60 cm) circular needles.

GAUGE:

Using US 6 (4 mm) needles, 20 stitches x 26 rows = 4 in (10 cm) over k2, p2 rib pattern. Adjust the needle size to get the correct tension.

As the pattern emerges on the collar, the alternating colors will look slightly misaligned, as shown below.

Add in CC1 (mustard) and work 3 rounds:

Round 5 (CC1) (increase): *yo, k11, yo, k1*, repeat from *to* to the end of the round (140 stitches).

Round 6 (CC1): *yo, k5, sl1, k2tog, psso, k5, yo, k1*, repeat from *to* to the end of the round.

Round 7 (CC1) (increase): *yo, k13, yo, k1*, repeat from *to* to the end of the round (160 stitches).

Add in CC2 (cherry) and work 2 rounds:

Round 8 (CC2): *yo, k6, sl1, k2tog, psso, k6, yo, k1*, repeat from *to* to the end of the round.

Round 9 (CC2) (increase): *yo, k15, yo, k1*, repeat from *to* to the end of the round (180 stitches).

Rejoin MC (ivory) and change to US 6 (4 mm) 24 in (60 cm) circular needle and work 3 rounds:

Round 10 (MC): *yo, k7, sl1, k2tog, psso, k7, yo, k1*, repeat from *to* to the end of the round.

Round 11 (MC) (increase): *yo, k17, yo, k1*, repeat from *to* to the end of the round (200 stitches).

Round 12 (MC): *yo, k8, sl1, k2tog, psso, k8, yo, k1*, repeat from *to* to the end of the round.

Add in CC3 (aqua) and work 3 rounds:

Round 13 (CC3) (increase): *yo, k19, yo, k1*, repeat from *to* to the end of the round (220 stitches).

Round 14 (CC3): *yo, k9, sl1, k2tog, psso, k9, yo, k1*, repeat from *to* to the end of the round.

Round 15 (CC3) (increase): *yo, k21, yo, k1*, repeat from *to* to the end of the round (240 stitches).

Add in CC4 (black) and work 2 rounds:

Round 16 (CC4): *yo, k10, sl1, k2tog, psso, k10, yo, k1*, repeat from *to* to the end of the round.

Round 17 (CC4) (increase): *yo, k23, yo, k1*, repeat from *to* to the end of the round (260 stitches).

Add in CC5 (hemp) and work 4 rounds:

Round 18 (CC5): *yo, k11, sl1, k2tog, psso, k11, yo, k1*, repeat from *to* to the end of the round.

Round 19 (CC5) (increase): *yo, k25, yo, k1*, repeat from *to* to the end of the round (280 stitches).

Round 20 (CC5): *yo, k12, sl1, k2tog, psso, k12, yo, k1*, repeat from *to* to the end of the round.

Round 21 (CC5) (increase): *yo, k27, yo, k1*, repeat from *to* to the end of the round (300 stitches).

Rejoin CC3 (cherry) and work 4 rounds:

Round 22 (CC3): *yo, k13, sl1, k2tog, psso, k13, yo, k1*, repeat from *to* to the end of the round.

Round 23 (CC3) (increase): *yo, k29, yo, k1*, repeat from *to* to the end of the round (320 stitches).

Round 24 (CC3): *yo, k14, sl1, k2tog, psso, k14, yo, k1*, repeat from *to* to the end of the round.

Round 25 (CC3) (increase): *yo, k31, yo, k1*, repeat from *to* to the end of the round (340 stitches).

Rejoin MC (ivory) and work 3 rounds:

Round 26 (MC): *yo, k15, sl1, k2tog, psso, k15, yo, k1*, repeat from *to* to the end of the round.

Round 27 (MC) (increase): *yo, k33, yo, k1*, repeat from *to* to the end of the round (360 stitches).

Round 28 (MC): *yo, k16, sl1, k2tog, psso, k16, yo, k1*, repeat from *to* to the end of the round.

Rejoin CC2 (mustard) and work 5 rounds:

Round 29 (CC2) (increase): *yo, k35, yo, k1*, repeat from *to* to the end of the round (380 stitches).

Round 30 (CC2): *yo, k17, sl1, k2tog, psso, k17, yo, k1*, repeat from *to* to the end of the round.

Round 31 (CC2) (increase): *yo, k37, yo, k1*, repeat from *to* to the end of the round (400 stitches).

Round 32 (CC2): *yo, k18, sl1, k2tog, psso, k18, yo, k1*, repeat from *to* to the end of the round.

Round 33 (CC2): knit.

Rejoin CC4 (black) and work 3 rounds:

Round 34 (CC4): *yo, k18, sl1, k2tog, psso, k18, yo, k1*, repeat from *to* to the end of the round.

Round 35 (CC4): knit.

Round 36 (CC4): *yo, k18, sl1, k2tog, psso, k18, yo, k1*, repeat from *to* to the end of the round.

Rejoin CC3 (aqua) and work 5 rounds:

Round 37 (CC3): knit.

Round 38 (CC3): *yo, k18, sl1, k2tog, psso, k18, yo, k1*, repeat from *to* to the end of the round.

Round 39 (CC3): knit.

Round 40 (CC3): *yo, k18, sl1, k2tog, psso, k18, yo, k1*, repeat from *to* to the end of the round.

Round 41 (CC3): knit.

Rejoin CC5 (hemp) and work 6 rounds:

Round 42 (CC5): *yo, k18, sl1, k2tog, psso, k18, yo, k1*, repeat from *to* to the end of the round.

Round 43 (CC5): knit.

Round 44 (CC5): *yo, k18, sl1, k2tog, psso, k18, yo, k1*, repeat from *to* to the end of the round.

Round 45 (CC5): knit.

Round 46 (CC5): *yo, k18, sl1, k2tog, psso, k18, yo, k1*, repeat from *to* to the end of the round.

Round 47 (CC5): knit.

Rejoin CC2 (cherry) and work 2 rounds:

Round 48 (CC2): *yo, k18, sl1, k2tog, psso, k18, yo, k1*, repeat from *to* to the end of the round.

Round 49 (CC2): knit.

Bind off loosely knitwise.

Using US 6 (4 mm) 14 in (35.5 cm) circular needle or US 6 (4 mm) straight needles and MC (ivory), begin the main body of the vest:

The body of this vest is worked entirely in k2, p2 rib. I recommend you separate the yarn into two balls and knit both sides (front and back) at once so that you can replicate the shaping easily. With the right side of the collar facing, using MC, pick up 40 stitches along the cast-on edge using one ball of yarn, and pick up another 40 stitches using the second ball (80 stitches in total).

Work 4 rows of k2, p2 rib, turning at the end of each row..

Increase at the end of next and every second row by kfb into the first and last stitches. Continue working this way, increasing every second row, until work measures 5¾ (7, 8¼) in (14.5, 17.75, 21 cm).

You should have 68 (76, 84) stitches for each front/back on your needles.

Continue to work straight in k2, p2 rib until work measures 8½ (9, 9½) in (21.5, 22.75, 24 cm) from where you picked up the stitches at the collar edge.

Increase at each end of next 6 rows, by kfb into first and last stitch (80, 88, 96 stitches for each front/back).

Change to US 6 (4 mm) 24 in (60 cm) circular needle and with right sides facing, start working in rounds; use a marker, if using, and slip on every round:

Note: What was the right side of the collar, will now become the inside of the body. This is important to remember when you join the contrast colors in so that the join is not apparent. Roll the collar over and make sure you know which will be the right side, before you join in the colors.

Work 3 rounds k2, p2 rib in MC (ivory).

Change to CC5 (hemp) and knit 1 round.

Work another 19 (21, 23) rounds k2, p2 rib in CC5.

Change to CC3 (aqua) and knit 1 round.

Work another 15 (17, 19) rounds k2, p2 rib in CC3.

Change to CC1 (mustard) and knit 1 round.

Work 9 (11, 13) rounds k2, p2 rib in CC1.

Change to CC4 (black) and knit 1 round.

Work 8 (10, 12) rounds k2, p2 rib in CC4.

Change to CC2 (cherry) and knit 1 round.

Work 6 (6, 8) rounds k2, p2 rib in CC2.

Bind off in k2, p2 rib pattern.

Finished length from the armhole is 9¾ (11, 12½) in (24.75, 28, 31.75 cm). You can adjust it by adding or subtracting more rows to each section above. Adding or subtracting 8 rows will make it approximately 1¼ in (3 cm) longer or shorter.

TO FINISH

Break off yarn leaving an 8 in (20 cm) tail and tie off securely. Using a darning needle, weave yarn tails into stitches on the wrong side.

COZY HAT

Knitted flat and in the round   Level: Easy

Hats that incorporate earflaps have always been popular with skiers and other outdoors people. I wanted to create one that didn't simply have a couple of triangle shapes tacked on each side to cover the ears. Although I have kept the colors neutral, this hat lends itself to almost any color combination, even some different colored stripes. Let your imagination go wild. I couldn't resist adding some braided tassels and an oversized pompom.

FINISHED MEASUREMENTS:

One size to fit head circumference between 21 in (53.5 cm) and 23 in (58.5 cm).

YARN:

Naturally Harmony Aran 10 ply

100% New Zealand merino; 1.76 oz (50 g) skein; 115 yds (105 m)

Naturally Baby Natural 8 ply

100% New Zealand rare breed Arapawa merino; 1.76 oz (50 g) skein; 115 yds (105 m)

Main Color (MC)
1 skein: Naturally Harmony 10 ply, shade #801

Contrast Color (CC)
1 skein: Naturally Baby Natural, shade #100

NEEDLES:

US 6 (4 mm) straight needles and US 6 (4 mm) double-pointed needles

GAUGE:

Using US 6 (4 mm) needles, 19 stitches x 26 rows = 4 in (10 cm) over stocking stitch pattern. Adjust the needle size as needed to get the correct tension.

To start, using MC, cast on 60 stitches with US 6 (4 mm) straight needles:

Foundation row: *k1, p1*, repeat from *to* to the end of the row.

Row 1: sl1, *k1, p1*, repeat from *to* to the end of the row.

Rows 2: sl1, *p1, k1*, repeat from *to* to the end of the row.

Repeat rows 1 & 2, 10 more times.

Row 23: knit.

Row 24 (increase): kfb, knit to last stitch, kfb (62 stitches).

Row 25: purl.

Repeat rows 24 & 25, 4 more times (70 stitches).

Change to US 6 (4 mm) double-pointed needles, distributing the stitches evenly between 3 needles, and start working in the round alternating between MC (natural) and CC (taupe):

Place marker, if using, and slip every round.

Round 1 (CC): knit.

Round 2 (CC): purl.

Rounds 3–8 (MC): knit.

Round 9 (CC): knit.

Round 10 (CC): purl.

Rounds 11–15 (MC): knit.

Round 16 (CC): knit.

Round 17 (CC): purl.

Rounds 18–21 (MC): knit.

Round 22 (CC): knit.

Round 23 (CC): purl.

Start decreasing for top of the hat:

Round 24 (MC) (decrease): *k8, k2tog*, repeat from *to* to the end of the round (63 stitches).

Rounds 25–27 (MC): knit.

Round 28 (CC): knit.

Round 29 (CC): purl.

Round 30 (MC): *k7, k2tog*, repeat from *to* to the end of the round (56 stitches).

Rounds 31–33 (MC): knit.

Round 34 (CC): knit.

Round 35 (CC): purl.

Round 36 (MC): *k6, k2tog*, repeat from *to* to the end of the round (49 stitches).

Round 37 (MC): knit.

Round 38 (CC): knit.

Round 39 (CC): purl.

Round 40 (MC): *k5, k2tog*, repeat from *to* to the end of the round (42 stitches).

Round 41 (MC): knit.

Round 42 (CC): knit.

Round 43 (CC): purl.

Round 44 (MC): *k4, k2tog*, repeat from *to* to the end of the round (35 stitches).

Round 45 (MC): knit.

Round 46 (CC): knit.

Round 47 (CC): purl.

Round 48 (CC): *k3, k2tog*, repeat from *to* to the end of the round (30 stitches).

Round 49 (CC): k2tog, repeat to the end of the round (15 stitches).

Break off yarn and pull through the stitches on the needles and tie off tightly.

TO MAKE THE BRAIDS

Cut 9 pieces of MC yarn 14 in (35.5 cm) long. Using a darning needle feed them through one front corner of the cast-on edge of the moss stitch border. Adjust them so that there is equal length on both sides. Divide the strands into three groups (six strands in each) and make a braid 3 in (7.5 cm) long. To finish, tie into a tight knot and trim the yarn ends to make them even. Repeat on the other front corner of the hat.

TO MAKE THE POMPOM USING CC

Cut two 4 in (10 cm) circles out of cardboard. Make a 1 in (2.5 cm) hole in the middle of both. Place one circle on top of the other and wrap the yarn evenly around both, going through the center hole each time. Keep going until you cannot get any more yarn through the middle. Cut a length of yarn approximately 20 in (50.75 cm) long and fold it over so you have a double strand. Take a sharp pair of pointed scissors and cut the outside edge of the circle of yarn by slipping the points in between the cardboard circles and, at the same time, keep a firm hold on the middle of the flat circle of yarn to stop it unraveling. Once the yarn is cut around the entire circumference, place the doubled-over length of yarn in between the cardboard circles and pull as tight as you can without breaking the yarn. Tie a knot and then wrap the tails around the center a few more times and tie off securely. Finally, pull the cardboard circles away from the yarn and you should have a fluffy pompom. Trim the surface to tidy up any uneven long strands, but leave the long yarn tails that you used to tie it off as you will use these to sew the pompom on the hat.

TO FINISH

Break off yarn leaving an 8 in (20 cm) tail and tie off securely. Using a darning needle, weave yarn tails into stitches on the wrong side. Use the yarn tails of the pompom to sew it in place.

WINTER WARMTH MITTENS

Knitted in the round   Level: Easy–Intermediate

FINISHED MEASUREMENTS:

Small: 11½ in (29.25 cm) long with cuff unfolded, 8½ in (21.5 cm) long with cuff folded and 4 in (10 cm) at the widest part

Medium: 12 in (30.5 cm) long with cuff unfolded, 9 in (22.75 cm) long with cuff folded and 4½ in (11.5 cm) at widest part

Large: 12½ in (31.75 cm) long with cuff unfolded, 9½ in (24 cm) long with cuff folded and 5 in (12.75 cm) at the widest part

YARN:

Lion Brand LB Collection Superwash Merino 8 ply

100% superwash merino; 3.5 oz (100 g) skein; 306 yds (280 m)

Main Color (MC) 1 skein: shade #113 Cherry

Contrast Color 1 (CC1) 1 skein: shade #170 Dijon

Contrast Color 2 (CC2) 1 skein: shade #102 Aqua

Note: If using smaller skeins (1.76 oz/50 g) you will still only need one of each color. The total weight of this pair of mittens is 2.3 oz (65 g).

NEEDLES:

US 3 (3.25 mm) set of double-pointed needles

. . . cont. next page

These warm mittens are made of a tight knitted fabric that really does not look like it is knitted at all. It's a clever stitch that uses three colors and I have become very fond of it. I have chosen primary colors that are just a little different — aqua rather than blue, mustard instead of yellow and bright cherry red. I used a superwash merino from Lion Brand, which is closer to a 5 ply in thickness, so substituting another 8 ply yarn may make the sizes too big and you should check the gauge first. It comes in large skeins (3.5 oz/100 g) and I was able to make these mittens and a vest (page 61), hat (page 72) and fingerless gloves (page 45) from six skeins in total (one in each color).

To start one mitten, using MC cast on 48 (56, 64) stitches with US 3 (3.25 mm) double-pointed needles:

Distribute the stitches evenly across three of the needles and start working in the round.

Work k2, p2 rib for 4 in (10 cm).

Add in the contrast colors to begin pattern and main part of mittens:

Place marker, if using, and slip on every round.

Pattern round 1 (MC): *k1, yf, sl1 and carry yarn across front of work, yb*, repeat from *to* to the last stitch.

Pattern round 2 (CC1): *yf, sl1 and carry yarn across front of work, yb, k1*, repeat from *to* to the last stitch.

Pattern round 3 (CC2): *k1, yf, sl1 and carry yarn across front of work, yb*, repeat from *to* to the last stitch.

Pattern round 4 (MC): *yf, sl1 and carry yarn across front of work, yb, k1*, repeat from *to* to the last stitch.

Pattern round 5 (CC1): *k1, yf, sl1 and carry yarn across front of work, yb*, repeat from *to* to the last stitch.

Pattern round 6 (CC2): *yf, sl1 and carry yarn across front of work, yb, k1*, repeat from *to* to the last stitch.

GAUGE:

Using US 3 (3.25 mm) needles, 26 stitches x 48 rows = 4 in (10 cm) over pattern. Adjust the needle size to get the correct tension.

These 6 rounds form the pattern and you should start to see it emerge after 6–12 rounds.

Repeat these 6 rounds until work measures 6½ (7, 7½) in (16.5, 17.75, 19 cm).

Separate for thumb:

Work 18 (21, 24) stitches in pattern, place next 12 (14, 16) stitches onto stitch holder, work next 18 (21, 24) stitches in pattern.

Keep working on these 36 (42, 48) stitches, keeping the pattern correct, until your work measures 11 (11½, 12) in (28, 29.25, 30.5 cm) from the cast-on edge.

Working in MC only, decrease for top of mitten:

Round 1 (decrease): *sl1, k1, psso*, repeat from *to* to the end of the round (18, 21, 24 stitches).

Round 2 (decrease): *sl1, k1, psso, k1*, repeat from *to* to the end of the round (12, 14, 16 stitches).

Round 3 (decrease): *sl1, k1, psso*, repeat from *to* to end of the round (6, 7, 8 stitches).

Pull yarn through stitches on needle, pull tightly and tie off on reverse.

Working on the 12 (14, 16) stitches on the holder, rejoin MC to make the thumb:

Place stitches onto double-pointed needles and pick up and knit 6 (7, 8) stitches along the thumb edge of the main part of the mitten (18, 21, 24 stitches). Place marker, if using, and slip on every round.

Rounds 1–8: knit.

Round 9 (decrease): *k4 (5, 6), k2tog*, repeat from *to* twice (15, 18, 21 stitches).

Rounds 10–13: knit.

Round 14 (decrease): *k3 (4, 5), k2tog*, repeat from *to* twice (12, 15, 18 stitches).

Rounds 15–18: knit.

Round 19 (decrease): *k2 (3, 4), k2tog*, repeat from *to* twice (9, 12, 15 stitches).

Round 20: knit.

Round 21 (decrease): *k1 (2, 3), k2tog*, repeat from *to* twice (6, 9, 12 stitches).

Stop here for small size, break yarn and pull yarn through stitches on needle, pull tightly and tie off on reverse.

Continue for medium and large sizes:

Round 22 (decrease): *k1, k2tog*, repeat from *to* twice (6, 8 stitches).

Break yarn and pull yarn through stitches on needle, pull tightly and tie off on reverse.

Repeat for second mitten.

TO FINISH

Break off yarn leaving an 8 in (20 cm) tail and tie off securely. Using a darning needle, weave yarn tails into stitches on the wrong side. You may need to place a few stitches at the base of the thumb, where it joins the main part of the mitten, if the stitches are stretched wide apart.

SQUARE PLAY REVERSIBLE HAT

Knitted in the round   Level: Intermediate–Advanced

FINISHED MEASUREMENTS:

Small: up to 19½ in (49.5 cm) head circumference

Large: up to 23½ in (60 cm) head circumference

YARN:

Lion Brand LB Collection Superwash Merino 8 ply

100% superwash merino; 3.5 oz (100 g) skein; 306 yds (280 m)

Main Color (MC)
1 skein: shade #153 Night Sky

Contrast Color 1 (CC1)
1 skein: shade #113 Cherry

Contrast Color 2 (CC2)
1 skein: shade #170 Dijon

Contrast Color 3 (CC3)
1 skein: shade #102 Aqua

Contrast Color 4 (CC4)
1 skein: shade #123 Hemp

Note: If using smaller skeins (1.76 oz/50 g) you will still only need one of each color, although you may want to purchase an extra skein of the background color that you choose. It is a little variable how much yarn is used by different people with a Fair Isle pattern like this.

. . . cont. next page

This fully reversible hat is double-layered and is incredibly warm and cozy. I have chosen three strong primary colors and partnered them with a black and neutral shade of the same yarn for maximum contrast. The inside layer is a completely different pattern (see page 75), but you could use the same pattern on both sides or knit it with a single contrast color, or even a variegated yarn. I used the LB Collection superwash merino from Lion Brand, which is closer to a 5 ply in thickness so substituting another 8 ply yarn may make the sizes too big and you should check the gauge first. It comes in large skeins (3.5 oz/100 g). I was able to make this hat and a vest (page 61), fingerless gloves (page 45) and mittens (page 69) from six skeins in total (one in each color).

To start the outer layer of the hat, using MC (black), cast on 96 (120) stitches with US 6 (4 mm) double-pointed needles or circular needle:

Distribute the stitches evenly across three of the needles and start working in the round. Do not turn your work, keep knitting around the circle, with the right side of your work facing you. Place marker, if using, and slip on every round.

Rounds 1–6 (MC): knit.

Rounds 7–16 (MC & CC1): Work these 10 rounds according to chart 1 (next page). Carry the yarn loosely behind the stitches as you work.

Rounds 17–18 (MC): knit.

Rounds 19–28 (MC & CC2): Work these 10 rounds according to chart 1. Carry the yarn loosely behind the stitches as you work.

Rounds 29–30 (MC): knit.

Rounds 31–40 (MC & CC3): Work these 10 rounds according to chart 1. Carry the yarn loosely behind the stitches as you work.

NEEDLES:

US 6 (4 mm) set of double-pointed needles or US 6 (4 mm) 16 in (40 cm) circular needle

GAUGE:

Using US 6 (4 mm) needles, 20 stitches x 28 rows = 4 in (10 cm) over first pattern (boxes on MC background). Adjust the needle size to get the correct tension.

Outside pattern worked over 12 stitches and 10 rounds.

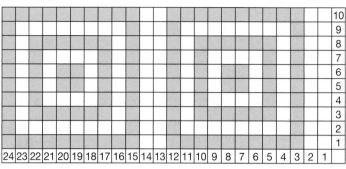

CHART 1 SYMBOLS

	knit MC
	knit CC

Rounds 41–42 (MC): knit.

Rounds 43–52 (MC & CC4): Work these 10 rounds according to chart 1. Carry the yarn loosely behind the stitches as you work.

Rounds 53–64 (MC): knit.

To bind off, split the stitches evenly onto 2 needles. With the right sides of your work together, hold both the needles side by side and, using a third needle, pick up and knit 1 stitch together from each needle. Bind off loosely knitwise.

Break off yarn leaving an 8 in (20 cm) tail and tie off securely. Using a darning needle, weave yarn tails into stitches on the wrong side. (i.e. between the layers of the hat).

To complete the inside layer:

Using CC4 (neutral), with right-side facing and US 6 (4 mm) double-pointed needles, pick up and knit 96 (120) stitches along the cast-on edge.

Rounds 1–6 (CC4): knit.

Rounds 7–26 (all colors): Work these 20 rounds according to chart 2. Carry the yarn loosely behind the stitches as you work.

Repeat rounds 7–26 once more.

Rounds 47–54: keep working in pattern, repeat rounds 1–8 of pattern.

Rounds 55–64 (CC4): knit.

To bind off, split the stitches evenly onto 2 needles. With the right sides of your work together, hold both the needles side by side and, using a third needle, pick up and knit 1 stitch together from each needle. Bind off loosely knitwise.

Break off yarn leaving an 8 in (20 cm) tail and tie off securely. Using a darning needle, weave yarn tails into stitches on the wrong side. (i.e. between the layers of the hat).

CHART 2

Inside pattern worked over 6 stitches and 20 rounds (colors as per photo).

TO FINISH

Make sure the ends of the yarn are tied off securely and woven between the layers. The top of this hat is folded over to create a square. To do this, lay the hat flat and pick up one end of the final bind-off edge and fold this over to the middle of the bind off edge and pin in place. Repeat for the opposite corner. The ends of the bind-off row should form the point of a triangle and these should meet in the middle of the hat. Using a darning needle, stitch securely in place. Repeat this process for both sides of the hat. Push one side inside the other to create the final shape.

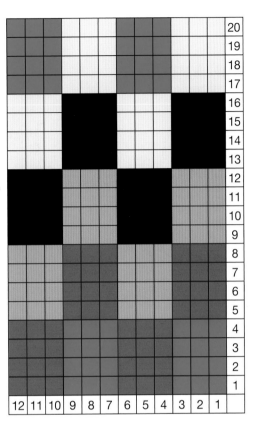

ALL NATURAL CABLED BEANIE

Knitted flat and in the round | Level: Intermediate

I really love the natural feel of this beanie. It's a no-nonsense, keep warm kind of hat with a little touch of style provided by the sideways cable brim. The simple stocking stitch upper section creates the contrast to make this cabled band, designed to mimic basketwork, stand out. The impact is further highlighted by the natural shade of pure merino yarn used: it's an archetypal outdoor hat. Although I love the tonal shades of this yarn, any other solid color would work, but I would not be tempted to use a highly colored yarn for this style — this hat is all about simple structure.

FINISHED MEASUREMENTS:

Small: 21 in (53.5 cm) head circumference

Medium: 22 in (55.75 cm) head circumference

Large: 23 in (58.5 cm) head circumference

YARN:

Skeinz Heritage Silver Lining 8 ply

Pure New Zealand rare breed 100% merino yarn; 1.76 oz (50 g) skein; 119 yds (109 m)

2 skeins: shade Clifton Stone

NEEDLES:

US 6 (4 mm) straight needles and set of double-pointed needles, plus a cable needle

GAUGE:

Using US 6 (4 mm) needles, 19 stitches x 26 rows = 4 in (10 cm) over stocking stitch pattern. Adjust the needle size as needed to get the correct tension.

To start, cast on 24 stitches with US 6 (4 mm) straight needles:

Rows 1–8: *k2, p2*, repeat from *to* to the end.

Row 9 (cable row): *sl2 onto cn, hold cn at front, k2, p2, k2 from cn, p2*, repeat from *to* 2 more times.

Rows 10–16: *k2, p2*, repeat from *to* to the end.

Row 17 (cable row): k2, p2, *sl2 onto cn, hold cn at front, k2, p2, k2 from cn, p2*, repeat from *to* once more, k2, p2.

Rows 18–24: *k2, p2*, repeat from *to* to the end.

Repeat rows 9–24 until work measures 21 (22, 23) in (53.5, 55.75, 58.5 cm) ending with a cable row.

Bind off loosely in double rib (k2, p2) pattern.

You should have 13 (14, 15) cable rows in total.

With right sides facing, sew the cast-on and cast-off edges together to create the circular band.

To make the top of the hat, with US 6 (4 mm) double-pointed needles, pick up and knit 81 (90, 99) stitches around the purl edge of the band with right-side facing:

Rounds 1–18: knit.

Round 19 (decrease): *k7, sl1, k1, psso*, repeat from *to* to the end of the round (72, 80, 88 stitches).

Round 20: knit.

Round 21 (decrease): *k6, sl1, k1, psso*, repeat from *to* to the end of the round (63, 70, 77 stitches).

Round 22: knit.

Round 23 (decrease): *k5, sl1, k1, psso*, repeat from *to* to the end of the round (54, 60, 66 stitches).

Round 24: knit.

Round 25 (decrease): *k4, sl1, k1, psso*, repeat from *to* to the end of the round (45, 50, 55 stitches).

Round 26: knit.

Round 27 (decrease): *k3, sl1, k1, psso*, repeat from *to* to the end of the round (36, 40, 44 stitches).

Round 28: knit.

Round 29 (decrease): *k2, sl1, k1, psso*, repeat from *to* to the end of the round (27, 30, 33 stitches).

Round 30: knit.

Round 31 (decrease): *k1, sl1, k1, psso*, repeat from *to* to the end of the round (18, 20, 22 stitches).

Round 32: knit.

Round 33 (decrease): *sl1, k1, psso*, repeat from *to* to the end of the round (9, 10, 11 stitches).

Break off yarn and thread through remaining stitches on the needle. Pull tight and tie off securely.

TO FINISH

Break off yarn leaving an 8 in (20 cm) tail and tie off securely. Using a darning needle, weave yarn tail into stitches on the wrong side.

ZIG-ZAG SCARF

Knitted flat   Level: Easy–Intermediate

FINISHED MEASUREMENTS:

70 in (177.75 cm) in length, and 9 in (22.75 cm) wide

YARN:

4 Seasons 100% merino 4 ply

1.76 oz (50 g) skein; 148 yds (135 m)

Contrast Color 1 (CC1) 2 skeins: shade #11 Donkey

Contrast Color 2 (CC2) 2 skeins: shade #10 Black

NEEDLES:

US 3 (3.25 mm) straight needles

GAUGE:

Using US 3 (3.25 mm) straight needles, 29 stitches x 29 rows = 4 in (10 cm) over chevron pattern. Adjust the needle size as needed to get the correct tension.

This geometric scarf uses two contrasting color yarns in a simple chevron pattern to create the uneven, yet symmetric striped effect. The color balance in this scarf shifts from the ends to the center — it starts out as a brown scarf with black highlights and then gradually becomes a black scarf with brown highlights around the neck area. As you finish the scarf, the color transitions are reversed and it ends up being a brown scarf with black highlights again. I think this would look really amazing in two similar pastel shades, but I have used stronger colors as this scarf was designed for a more masculine look. It is worked lengthways, so you can make it longer or shorter as you desire by adding in rows (symmetrically of course!).

To start the scarf, using CC1 (brown), cast on 65 stitches with US 3 (3.25 mm) straight needles:

This pattern is made of 2 alternating rows — a plain knit row and a pattern row.

Knit row: sl1, knit remaining stitches.

Note: by slipping the first stitch of every row, a neater edge is achieved.

Pattern row: sl1, k1, k2tog, *k8, yo, k1, yo, k8, sl1, k2tog, psso*, repeat from *to* once more, k8, yo, k1, yo, k8, sl1, k1, psso, k2.

Alternating the knit row and the pattern row:

Work 20 rows in CC1 (brown).

Work 4 rows in CC2 (black).

Work 18 rows in CC1.

Work 6 rows in CC2.

Work 16 rows in CC1.

Work 8 rows in CC2.

Work 14 rows in CC1.

Work 10 rows in CC2.

Work 12 rows in CC1.

Work 12 rows in CC2.
Work 10 rows in CC1.
Work 14 rows in CC2.
Work 8 rows in CC1.
Work 16 rows in CC2.
Work 6 rows in CC1.
Work 18 rows in CC2.
Work 4 rows in CC1.
Work 20 rows in CC2.
Work 4 rows in CC1.
Work 18 rows in CC2.
Work 6 rows in CC1.
Work 16 rows in CC2.
Work 8 rows in CC1.
Work 14 rows in CC2.
Work 10 rows in CC1.
Work 12 rows in CC2.
Work 12 rows in CC1.
Work 10 rows in CC2.

Work 14 rows in CC1.
Work 8 rows in CC2.
Work 16 rows in CC1.
Work 6 rows in CC2.
Work 18 rows in CC1.
Work 4 rows in CC2.
Work 20 rows in CC1.
Bind off loosely knitwise in CC1.

TO FINISH

Make sure the ends of the yarn are tied off and woven in on the wrong side. I have made a single crochet edge along both long edges of my scarf — it's not necessary, but I wanted to finish the edge in black. To do this, use a crochet hook US E-4 (3.5 mm) size and, starting at the first CC2 stripe, work one single crochet (British double crochet) into each stitch along the edge until you reach the same stripe at the other end of the scarf. Repeat on both long sides.

WOMAN'S CABLE VEST

Knitted flat   Level: Intermediate

This pattern looks harder than it is! Essentially the central cable segment, which goes all the way from the front to the back and includes the collar, is made as one piece. Once this is completed, you pick up the edges of the cable section and work sideways across the garment, completing both the front and back at the same time. There is a similar man's vest on page 23, which has more shaped armholes and a different cable pattern. I really like the dramatic effect of this color scheme, although the cable does not have to be such a strong contrast color. In the past, I have been put off by these types of cable patterns, but they really are surprisingly easy.

FINISHED MEASUREMENTS:

Small/medium: 39 in (99 cm) chest/hips and 35 in (89 cm) long (from shoulder)

Large: 45 in (114.25 cm) chest/hips and 35 in (89 cm) long (from shoulder)

YARN:

Naturally Harmony Colour DK

100% pure New Zealand merino; 1.76 oz (50 g) skein; 145 yds (132.5 m)

Naturally Merino/Silk DK

70% merino; 20% silk; 10% nylon; 1.76 oz (50 g) skein; 137 yds (125 m)

Main Color (MC) 3 skeins: Naturally Merino/ Silk, shade 60

Contrast Color (CC) 5 (6) skeins: Naturally Harmony Colour, shade 54

NEEDLES:

US 6 (4 mm) straight needles and US 5 (3.75 mm) 24 in (60 cm) circular needles, plus a cable needle

GAUGE:

Using US 5 (3.75 mm) needles, 20 stitches x 28 rows = 4 in (10 cm) over stocking stitch used for the body. Adjust needle size as needed to get correct tension.

To start, using CC (pink) cast on 28 stitches with US 6 (4 mm) straight needles:

Row 1: p2, k24, p2.

Row 2: k2, p24, k2.

Repeat rows 1 & 2, 5 more times.

Row 13 (cable row): p2, sl6 stitches onto cn, hold at front, k6 from left-hand needle, k6 from cn, sl6 stitches onto cn, hold at back, k6 from left-hand needle, k6 from cn, p2.

Row 14: as row 2.

Repeat rows 1 & 2, 6 times.

Row 27 (cable row): as row 13.

Repeat rows 14–27, 9 times.

Your work should measure 18 in (45.75 cm). If you want to adjust the length, do so now, but remember this will affect the number of stitches you pick up later on.

Divide for the neck:

Row 1: k2, k24, k2.

Row 2: p2, k24, p2.

Row 3: k2, k24, k2.

Repeat rows 2 & 3, 5 more times.

Work on first 14 stitches only, to create left-hand collar.

Row 14 (cable row): p2, sl6 stitches onto cn, hold at front, k6 from left-hand needle, k6 from cn, turn. Place remaining stitches onto a stitch holder.

Row 15: p12, k2.

Row 16: p2, k12.

Row 17: p12, k2.

Repeat rows 16 &17, 5 more times.

Row 28 (cable row): p2, sl6 stitches onto cn, hold at front, k6 from left-hand needle, k6 from cn, turn.

Repeat rows 15–28, 6 times.

Return to right-hand collar, rejoin yarn and move the stitches on the holder onto a straight needle:

Row 14 (cable row): sl6 stitches onto cn, hold at back, k6 from left-hand needle, k6 from cn, p2, turn.

Row 15: k2, p12.

Row 16: k12, p2.

Row 17: k2, p12.

Repeat rows 16 &17, 5 more times.

Row 28 (cable row): sl6 stitches onto cn, hold at back, k6 from left-hand needle, p2, turn.

Repeat rows 15–28, 6 times.

With right sides facing, join the two sides of the collar together again:

Back row 1 (cable row): p2, sl6 stitches onto cn, hold at front, k6 from left-hand needle, k6 from cn, sl6 stitches onto cn, hold at back, k6 from left-hand needle, k6 from cn, p2.

Back row 2: k2, p24, k2.

Back row 3: p2, k24, p2.

Back row 4: k2, p24, k2.

Repeat back rows 3 & 4, 5 times (rows 5–14).

Repeat back rows 1–14 until your work measures 28 in (71 cm) from the top neck edge of the back (where you rejoined the two cable sides). If you have adjusted the front length, remember to adjust the back length by the same amount.

Bind off loosely, knitwise.

To make the sides, using CC (pink) and US 5 (3.75 mm) circular needle, pick up and knit 290 stitches along the edge of the cable piece you have just completed:

Use the circular needle like straight needles, turning at the end of each row.

Row 1 (CC): purl.

Break off CC and join in MC (black).

Row 2 (MC): knit.

Row 3 (MC): purl.

Repeat rows 2 & 3, 3 more times.

Rows 10 & 11 (MC): knit.

Rejoin CC, but do not break off the MC yarn.

Row 12 (CC): knit.

Break off CC yarn.

Do not turn. Return to the start of the row, where you left the MC yarn and continue knitting with the MC yarn going the same way you did for the last row worked.

Row 13 (MC): knit.

Repeat rows 1–13, 3 times for small/medium size and 4 times for large size.

Work 8 rows stocking stitch (one row purl, one row knit) as if using straight needles.

Your work should measure 8½ in (21.5 cm) for small/medium size and 9¾ in (24.75 cm) from where the MC plain knitting started.

Final row (MC): purl 95 stitches, bind off next 100 stitches loosely, purl to the end of the row. With the right sides together, hold the two ends of the circular needle side by side and, using a third needle, pick up and knit together one stitch from each needle and, at the same time, bind off knitwise loosely to form the side seam.

Repeat for the other side.

TO FINISH

Break off yarn leaving an 8 in (20 cm) tail and tie off securely. Using a darning needle, weave yarn tails into stitches on the wrong side.

SLOUCH BEANIE

Knitted in the round   Level: Easy

This textured rib beanie is quick to knit up and will suit almost anyone. It's a 'throw in your bag' kind of hat that you can pull out for any occasion and the ribbed pattern means it will keep its shape. The rib can be folded up or left longer. This is a simple k1, p1 rib pattern but it is slightly raised because you work every second stitch into the row below.

FINISHED MEASUREMENTS:

One size: fits 19¼ in (48.75 cm) to 23 in (58.5 cm) head circumference — the rib pattern means it stretches and I have used a merino yarn with 20% silk that gives it a shine.

YARN:

Skeinz Burlesque DK

75% merino, 25% tussah silk; 1.76 oz (50 g) skein; 106 yds (96 m)

Contrast Color 1 (CC1)
1 skein: shade #857 Blaurot

Contrast Color 2 (CC2)
1 skein: shade #850 Gothic

NEEDLES:

US 6 (4 mm) set of double-pointed needles or a 16 in (40 cm) circular needle

GAUGE:

Using US 6 (4 mm) needles, 14 stitches x 22 rows = 4 in (10 cm) over band rib pattern. Adjust the needle size as needed to get the correct tension.

To start the band of the hat, using CC1 (purple), cast on 80 stitches with US 6 (4 mm) double-pointed needles or circular needle.

Place marker, if using, and slip on every round.

Round 1 (CC1): (k1, p1) to the end.

Round 2 (CC1): (k1b, p1) to the end.

Round 3 (CC1): (k1, p1b) to the end.

Repeat rounds 2 & 3 until your work measures 3¼ in (8.25 cm).

To start the main body of the hat, join CC2 (black) and work the following patterns with each color:

Round 1 (CC2): knit.

Round 2 (CC2): (k1b, p1) to the end.

Repeat rounds 1 & 2, 3 more times (rounds 3–8).

Round 9 (CC1): knit.

Round 10 (CC1): (k1b, p1) to the end.

Repeat rounds 9 & 10, once more (rounds 11–12).

Round 13 (CC2): knit.

Round 14 (CC2): (k1b, p1) to the end.

Repeat rounds 13 & 14, 6 more times (rounds 15–26).

Round 27 (CC1): knit.

Round 28 (CC1): (k1b, p1) to the end.

Repeat rounds 27 & 28, twice more (rounds 29–32).

Round 33 (CC2): knit.

Round 34 (CC2): (k1b, p1) to the end.

Repeat rounds 33 & 34, once more (rounds 35–36).

Round 37 (CC1): knit.

Round 38 (CC1): (k1b, p1) to the end.

Round 39 (CC2): knit.

Round 40 (CC2): (k1b, p1) to the end.

Repeat rounds 39 & 40, 8 times (rounds 41–56).

Round 57 (CC1): knit.

Round 58 (CC1): (k1b, p1) to the end.

Repeat rounds 57 & 58, once more (rounds 59–60).

Round 61 (CC2): knit.

Round 62 (CC2): (k1b, p1) to the end.

Repeat rounds 61 & 62, 2 times (rounds 63–66).

Start decreasing for crown. Change to double-pointed needles if using a circular needle:

Note: When you get to a corner stitch (sl1, k2tog, psso), substitute k1 for k1b.

Round 67 (CC2) (decrease): *k8, sl1, k2tog, psso, k9*, repeat from *to* to the end of the round (72 stitches).

Round 68 (CC2): (k1b, p1) to the end.

Round 69 (CC2) (decrease): *k7, sl1, k2tog, psso, k8*, repeat from *to* to the end of the round (64 stitches).

Round 70 (CC2): (k1b, p1) to the end.

Round 71 (CC2) (decrease): *k6, sl1, k2tog, psso, k7*, repeat from *to* to the end of the round (56 stitches).

Round 72 (CC2): *(k1b, p1) to the end of the round.

Round 73 (CC2) (decrease): *k5, sl1, k2tog, psso, k6*, repeat from *to* to the end of the round (48 stitches).

Round 74 (CC2): (k1b, p1) to the end of the round.

Round 75 (CC2) (decrease): *k4, sl1, k2tog, psso, k5*, repeat from *to* to the end of the round (40 stitches).

Round 76 (CC2): (k1b, p1) to the end of the round.

Round 77 (CC2) (decrease): *k3, sl1, k2tog, psso, k4*, repeat from *to* to the end of the round (32 stitches).

Round 78 (CC2) (decrease):*k2, sl1, k2tog, psso, k3*, repeat from *to* to the end of the round (24 stitches).

Round 79 (CC2) (decrease):*sl1, k2tog, psso*, repeat from *to* to the end of the round (8 stitches).

Break off yarn and pull tightly through the stitches on the needle.

TO FINISH

Make sure ends of yarn are tied off securely. Weave in yarn tails on wrong side.

WINTER FIRE BEANIE

Knitted in the round   Level: Easy

FINISHED MEASUREMENTS:

One size only: fits 19¼ in (48.75 cm) to 23 in (58.5 cm) head circumference. The rib pattern means it stretches and the yarn used is a merino blend with 20% nylon, which adds some extra stretch.

YARN:

Naturally Waikiwi 4 ply

55% merino, 20% nylon, 15% alpaca, 10% possum ; 1.76 oz (50 g) skein; 198 yds (181 m)

Patons Dreamtime 4 ply

100% merino; 1.76 oz (50 g) skein; 185 yds (169 m)

Main Color (MC)
1 skein: Naturally Waikiwi Prints, shade #465

Contrast Color 1 (CC1)
1 skein: Patons Dreamtime 4 ply, shade #2957 Donkey

Contrast Color 2 (CC2)
1 skein: Naturally Waikiwi, shade #420

NEEDLES:

US 10 (6 mm) set of double-pointed needles or a 16 in (40 cm) circular needle

GAUGE:

Using US 10 (6 mm) needles, 20 stitches x 24 rows = 4 in (10 cm) over rib pattern. Adjust the needle size as needed to get the correct tension.

This beanie is quick to knit up because it uses two strands of 4 ply yarn worked together. The whole hat is made in a simple rib pattern that is offset in each stripe. The effect is enhanced by the different colored stripes, which are achieved by mixing different yarns. One variegated yarn is used for the whole hat, but the stripes are created by different plain color yarns (selected from the variegated colors) knitted together with the main variegated yarn.

To start the hat, using a strand of MC (variegated blue/red) and CC1 (brown) together, cast on 80 stitches with US 10 (6 mm) double-pointed needles or circular needle:

Place marker, if using, and slip on every round.

Rounds 1–11 (MC & CC1): *k1b, p1*, repeat from *to* to the end.

Break off CC1 yarn and work with a strand of MC and CC2 (blue) together.

Round 12 (MC & CC2): purl.

Rounds 13–21 (MC & CC2): *p1, k1b*, repeat from *to* to the end.

Break off CC2 yarn. and work with a strand of MC and CC1 together.

Round 22 (MC & CC1): purl.

Round 23 (MC & CC1) (decrease): *sl1, k2tog, psso, p1, (k1b, p1) 6 times*, repeat from *to* to the end of the round (70 stitches)

Rounds 24–28 (MC & CC1): *k1b, p1*, repeat from *to* to the end.

Break off CC1 yarn and work with a strand of MC and CC2 together.

Round 29 (MC & CC2): purl.

Rounds 30–34 (MC & CC2): *p1,k1b*, repeat from *to* to the end.

Break off yarn and switch to working with a strand of MC and CC1 together.

Round 35 (MC & CC1): purl.

Change to double-pointed needles if using circular needle:

Row 36 (MC & CC1) (decrease): *sl1, k2tog, psso, p1, (k1b, p1) 5 times*, repeat from *to* to the end of the round (60 stitches)

Rounds 37–39 (MC & CC1): *k1b, p1*, repeat from *to* to the end.

Break off CC1 yarn and work with a strand of MC and CC2 together.

Round 40 (MC & CC2): purl.

Rounds 41–43 (MC & CC2): *p1, k1b*, repeat from *to* to the end.

Break off CC2 yarn and work with a strand of MC and CC1 together.

Round 44 (MC & CC1): purl.

Round 45 (MC & CC1): *k1b, p1*, repeat from *to* to the end.

Round 46 (MC & CC1) (decrease): *sl1, k1, psso*, repeat from *to* to the end of the round (30 stitches).

Break off CC1 yarn and work with a strand of MC and CC2 together.

Round 47 (MC & CC2): purl.

Round 48 (MC & CC2): *p1, k1b*, repeat from *to* to the end.

Round 49 (MC & CC2): *sl1, k1, psso*, repeat from *to* to the end of the round (15 stitches).

Break off CC2 yarn and work with a strand of MC and CC1 together.

Round 50 (MC & CC1): purl.

Round 51 (MC & CC1) (decrease): k1, *sl1, k1, psso*, repeat from *to* to the end of the round (8 stitches).

Break off both yarns and pull through remaining stitches on the needles.

Tie off securely.

TO FINISH

Weave in yarn tails carefully. Since this hat is fully reversible — one side has more obvious ridged joins, whereas on the other side they are more subtle — you can wear it whichever way you prefer.

WINTER FIRE SCARF

Knitted flat | Level: Intermediate

This extra-long, lightweight scarf uses two 4 ply yarns — one is highly variegated and the other a contrasting plain color. I love the look of variegated yarns when I see them in the store, but often the knitted end result is, for me anyway, less appealing. By mixing this highly multicolored yarn with a solid color, I have achieved a more random effect, which I think is the objective of variegated yarns anyway! This scarf is worked from one long edge to the other and uses a long circular needle to hold all of the stitches. The tassels are created by leaving a long tail at the start and finish of each row when you change colors. I intentionally made this scarf long and narrow — it is light enough to double over, or wrap around your neck and head to keep warm.

FINISHED MEASUREMENTS:

The scarf is 80 in (203 cm) in length and 6 in (15.25 cm) wide. You can increase the length by adding extra stitches (for every 6 in (15.25 cm) increase or decrease in length add or subtract 22 stitches).

YARN:

Naturally Waikiwi 4 ply

55% merino, 20% nylon, 15% alpaca, 10% possum; 1.76 oz (50 g) skein; 198 yds (181 m)

Main Color (MC)
1 skein: Naturally Waikiwi Prints, shade #465

Contrast Color (CC)
1 skein Naturally Waikiwi, shade #420

NEEDLES:

US 3 (3.25 mm) circular needle, at least 24 in (60 cm) in length

GAUGE:

Using US 3 (3.25 mm) needles, 15 stitches x 29 rows = 4 in (10 cm) over pattern. Adjust the needle size as needed to get the correct tension.

To start the scarf, using MC (variegated blue/red), cast on 299 stitches with a US 3 (3.25 mm) circular needle:

Row 1 (MC): knit.

Break off MC, join CC. Leave a long tail (8 in, 20 cm) on both yarns, as these will become the tassels. Do this every time you change yarns.

Row 2 (CC): k1, *yo, k2tog*, repeat from *to* to the end of the row.

Row 3 (CC): purl.

Row 4 (CC): knit.

Break off CC, join MC, leaving 8 in (20 cm) yarn tails.

Rows 5 & 6 (MC): purl.

Row 7 (MC): knit.

Row 8 (MC): purl.

Row 9-10: repeat rows 7 & 8.

Break off MC, join CC, leaving 8 in (20 cm) yarn tails.

Row 11 (CC): purl.

Row 12 (CC): knit.

Row 13 (CC): purl.

Row 14 (CC): k1, *yo, k2tog*, repeat from *to* to the end of the row.

Row 15 (CC): purl.

Row 16 (CC): knit.

Break off CC, join MC, leaving 8 in (20 cm) yarn tails.

Rows 17 & 18 (MC): knit.

Row 19 (MC): purl.

Row 20-21: repeat rows 18 & 19.

Break off MC, join CC, leaving 8 in (20 cm) yarn tails.

Rows 22 & 23 (CC): purl.

Row 24 (CC): k1, *yo, k2tog*, repeat from *to* to the end of the row.

Row 25 (CC): purl.

Break off CC, join MC, leaving 8 in (20 cm) yarn tails.

Rows 26 & 27 (MC): knit.

Row 28 (MC): purl.

Row 29 (MC): knit.

Break off MC, join CC, leaving 8 in (20 cm) yarn tails.

Row 30 (CC): knit.

Row 31 (CC): purl.

Row 32 (CC): k1, *yo, k2tog*, repeat from *to* to the end of the row.

Row 33 (CC): purl.

Break off CC, join MC, leaving 8 in (20 cm) yarn tails.

Rows 34 & 35 (MC): purl.

Row 36 (MC): knit.

Break off MC, join CC, leaving 8 in (20 cm) yarn tails.

Row 37 (CC): knit.

Row 38 (CC): k1, *yo, k2tog*, repeat from *to* to the end of the row.

Row 39 (CC): purl.

Break off CC, join MC, leaving 8 in (20 cm) yarn tails.

Rows 40 & 41 (MC): knit.

Row 42 (MC): purl.

Break off MC, join CC, leaving 8 in (20 cm) yarn tails.

Row 43 (CC): purl.

Row 44 (CC): k1, *yo, k2tog*, repeat from *to* to the end of the row.

Break off CC, join MC, leaving 8 in (20 cm) yarn tails.

Rows 45 & 46 (MC): knit.

Row 47 (MC): purl.

Break off MC, join CC, leaving 8 in (20 cm) yarn tails.

Row 48 (CC): purl.

Row 49 (CC): purl.

Row 50 (CC): k1,*yo, k2tog*, repeat from *to* to the end of the row.

Bind off purlwise, leaving 8 in (20 cm) yarn tail.

TO FINISH

Make sure ends of yarn are tied off securely. Starting at short edge, grasp five yarn tails and tie a simple knot firmly at the base. Continue across the edge of the scarf until all yarn tails are secure. Repeat for the other end. Trim fringe to make it even.

AT THE BEACH

WEATHERING THE STORM

FINGERLESS FAIR ISLE GLOVES

Knitted flat   Level: Easy

These gloves might be better described as wrist warmers as they are designed to have maximum finger and thumb movement while providing comforting warmth. They knit up really quickly and are the easiest glove pattern in this book since they are worked flat on straight needles. I wanted to include an easy glove pattern because although knitting in the round is easy once you master it, knitting with double-pointed needles for the first time can be a little bit tricky with small items such as gloves. These gloves use knit and purl rows to create a rib pattern and a simple Fair Isle design on the back of the hands. This subtle color contrast detail could be omitted completely or enhanced further by using a vibrant color scheme.

Before you start knitting, divide the main color (MC) skein into two balls. You will need two balls once you start the Fair Isle pattern, since there are rows of contrast only and you don't carry the main color across these.

To start the left hand, using MC (dark grey) cast on 39 (41, 43) stitches with US 6 (4 mm) straight needles:

LH row 1: knit.

LH rows 2 & 3: purl.

LH rows 4 & 5: knit.

LH row 6: purl.

Start Fair Isle pattern. Carry the contrast color loosely across the back of your work:

LH row 7: p16 MC, k2 MC, *k1 CC (beige), k1 MC,* repeat from *to* to last 7 stitches, k1 CC, join second ball of MC color, k2, p4 MC.

LH row 8: k4 MC, p2 MC, *p1 CC, p1 MC,* repeat from *to* to last 19 stitches, p1 CC, p2 MC, k16 MC.

LH row 9: k18 MC, k15 (17, 19) CC, k6 MC using second ball of yarn.

FINISHED MEASUREMENTS:

Small: 8 in (20 cm) long and 4¼ in (10.75 cm) wide

Medium: 8½ in (21.5 cm) long and 4¾ in (12 cm) wide

Large: 10 in (25.5 cm) long and 5¼ in (13.5 cm) wide

YARN:

Skeinz Heritage Silver Lining 8 ply

Pure New Zealand rare breed 100% merino yarn; 1.76 oz (50 g) skein; 119 yds (109 m)

Main Color (MC)
1 skein: shade Five Mile Bush

Contrast Color (CC)
½ skein: shade Clifton Stone

NEEDLES:

US 6 (4 mm) straight needles

GAUGE:

Using US 6 (4 mm) needles, 22 stitches x 28 rows = 4 in (10 cm) over Fair Isle pattern; 18 stitches x 24 rows = 4 in (10 cm) over horizontal rib pattern. Adjust the needle size as needed to get the correct tension.

LH row 10: p6 MC, p15 (17, 19) CC, p18 MC.

LH row 11: p16 MC, k2 MC, *k1 MC, k1 CC,* repeat from *to* to last 7 stitches, k3 MC, p4 MC.

LH row 12: k4 MC, p2 MC, *p1 MC, p1 CC,* repeat from *to* to last 19 stitches, p3 MC, k16 MC.

LH row 13: k18 MC, k15 (17, 19) CC, k6 MC using second ball of yarn.

LH row 14: p6 MC, p15 (17, 19) CC, p18 MC.

Repeat LH rows 7–14, 2 more times.

Then, repeat LH rows 7 & 8.

Continue working in main color only:

LH row 33: knit.

LH rows 34 & 35: purl.

LH row 36: knit.

Make hole for thumb:

LH row 37: k20, bind off 8 (9, 10) stitches knitwise, k11 (12, 13).

LH row 38: p11 (12, 13), turn, then cast on 8 (9, 10) stitches, turn and purl to the end.

LH row 39: purl.

LH rows 40 & 41: knit.

LH rows 42 & 43: purl.

Repeat LH rows 40 to 43, 4 (5, 6) more times.

Last LH row: knit.

Bind off loosely knitwise.

To start the right hand, using main color (MC), cast on 39 (41, 43) stitches with US 6 (4 mm) straight needles:

RH row 1: knit.

RH rows 2 & 3: purl.

RH rows 4 & 5: knit.

Repeat RH rows 2–5, 4 (5, 6) more times.

Purl 1 row.

Make hole for thumb:

RH row 27: p20, bind off 8 (9, 10) stitches purlwise, p11 (12, 13).

RH row 28: k11 (12, 13), turn and cast on 8 (9, 10) stitches, turn and knit to the end.

RH rows 29: knit.

RH rows 30 & 31: purl.

Start Fair Isle pattern by introducing contrast color (CC):

RH row 32: k18 MC, *k1 CC, k1 MC,* repeat from *to* to last 7 stitches, k1 CC, join second ball of MC, k6 MC.

RH row 33: k4 MC, p2 MC, *p1 CC, p1 MC,* repeat from *to* to last 19 stitches, p1 CC, p2 MC, k16 MC.

RH row 34: p16 MC, k2 MC, k15 (17, 19) CC, k2, p4 MC.

RH row 35: p6 MC, p15 (17, 19) CC, p18 MC.

RH row 36: k18 MC, *k1 MC, k1 CC,* repeat from *to* to last 7 stitches, k7 MC.

RH row 37: k4 MC, p2 MC, *p1 MC, k1 CC,* repeat from *to* to last 19 stitches, p3 MC, k16 MC.

RH row 38: p18 MC, k15 (17, 19) CC, k2 MC, p4 MC.

RH row 39: p6 MC, p15 (17, 19) CC, p18 MC.

Repeat RH rows 32–39, 2 more times.

Repeat RH rows 32 & 33.

Continue working in main color only:

RH row 58 & 59: knit.

RH rows 60 & 61: purl.

RH row 62: purl.

Bind off all stitches loosely knitwise.

TO FINISH

Break off yarn leaving an 8 in (20 cm) tail and tie off securely. Fold your work over, right sides facing and sew the cast-on and cast-off edges together. Using a darning needle, weave yarn tails into stitches on the wrong side.

HOUNDSTOOTH VEST

Knitted in the round and straight   Level: Intermediate

I have always loved the repeating houndstooth pattern — especially the classic black and white version — I find it almost mesmerizing. For this vest, the pattern is large and bold and the deep V at the front is even bolder. I have paired a grey natural-colored yarn with a muted wine color, both in pure merino 8 ply. I intentionally used slightly larger needles than recommended for this yarn as I wanted the effect to be soft and light. Often I find that when I make a Fair Isle pattern like this, that requires you to carry the yarn across the back of the work, the result is a tight gauge fabric that feels heavy to wear. This one feels soft and light, which is partly the larger needles and, of course, partly due to the soft merino yarn.

FINISHED MEASUREMENTS:

Small: bust 32–33 in (81.25–84 cm)

Medium: bust 36–37 in (91.5–94 cm)

Large: bust 40–41 in (101.5–104 cm)

YARN:

Cleckheaton Country Merino 8 ply

100% Australian merino; 1.76 oz (50 g) skein; 94 yds (86 m)

Main Color (MC) 5 (5, 6) skeins: shade #009 Red

Contrast Color (CC) 3 (3, 3) skeins: shade #2957 Donkey

NEEDLES:

US 8 (5 mm) approximately 16–20 in (40–50 cm) circular needle and a US 5 (3.75 mm) approximately 16–20 in (40–50 cm) circular needle

GAUGE:

Using US 8 (5 mm) needles, 19 stitches x 20 rows = 4 in (10 cm) over houndstooth pattern stitch. Adjust the needle size as needed to get the correct tension.

To start, using MC (wine), cast on 140 (150, 160) stitches with US 5 (3.75 mm) circular needle:

This pattern is worked in the round. Place marker, if using, and slip on every round. Do not turn the work at the end of each round, but keep going, with the right side always facing you.

Work 6 in (15.25 cm) in the following rib pattern, (p2, k3) repeat to the end.

Change to US 8 (5 mm) circular needle and begin main body:

Bind off the first 2 stitches (these should be purl stitches in the rib), knit to the end of the round (138, 148, 158 stitches).

Divide at the front and start working in rows:

For the remainder of the body, you will be using the circular needle as if you are using straight needles. Remember to turn at the end of each row. You will be working the stocking stitch according to the pattern (see chart on the next page) with a 4-stitch plain border. You will need to carry both yarns loosely across the back of the work as you alternate colors. Be careful not to pull this too tight or your work will not lay flat.

CHART SYMBOLS

☐	Main color (MC)
▨	Contrast color (CC)

Chart grid (worked over 10 stitches and 12 rows). Rows numbered 12–1 (bottom to top) on the right; columns numbered 10, 9, 8, 7, 6, 5, 4, 3, 2, 1 along the bottom.

As shown in chart above, the pattern is worked over 10 stitches and 12 rows, purl on wrong side of work and knit on right side.

Row 1: sl1, p3, purl next 130 (140, 150) stitches according to the pattern in the chart , p4.

Row 2: sl1, k3, knit next 130 (140, 150) stitches according to the pattern in the chart, k4.

Repeat these 2 rows, keeping pattern correct as per the chart, until your work measures 14 in (35.5 cm) for small and medium sizes and 15½ in (39.5 cm) for large size, ending with row 11 of pattern chart (i.e. purl row).

Divide for the armhole:

Keeping pattern correct, divide for the front and armholes.

Row 1 (decrease): sl1, k3, knit next 30 (30, 35) stitches according to the pattern in the chart, bind off next 5 stitches, knit next 60 (70, 70) stitches according to the pattern, bind off next 5 stitches, knit next 30 (30, 35) stitches according to the pattern, k4 (34, 34, 39 stitches for each front section and 60, 70, 70 stitches for back section).

Continue working on the back:

Back row 1 (decrease): sl1, p1, psso, pattern to last 2 stitches, p2tog (58, 68, 68 stitches).

Back row 2 (decrease): sl1, k1, psso, pattern to last 2 stitches, k2tog (56, 66, 66 stitches).

Stop decreasing at the armhole edge and work straight keeping pattern correct until work measures 27 (28½, 30) in (68.5, 72.5, 76.25 cm) from cast-on edge, ending with a purl row.

Back last row: Work 20 (25, 25) stitches in pattern, bind off 16 stitches knitwise, work remaining 20 (25, 25) stitches in pattern.

Place stitches onto stitch holder and return to complete front sections.

Rejoin yarn to the 34 (34, 39) stitches of the right front and start with a wrong side row:

Continue decreasing at armhole edge every row for 6 rows, then every alternate row.

Row 1 (decrease): p2tog, work next 28 (28, 33) stitches according to the pattern, p4 (33, 33, 38 stitches).

Row 2 (decrease): sl1, k3, work next 27 (27, 32) stitches according to the pattern, sl1, k1, psso (32, 32, 37 stitches).

Row 3 (decrease): p2tog, work next 26 (26, 31) stitches according to the pattern, p4 (31, 31, 36 stitches).

Row 4 (decrease): sl1, k3, work next 25 (25, 30) stitches according to the pattern, sl1, k1, psso (30, 30, 35 stitches).

Row 5 (decrease): p2tog, work next 24 (24, 29) stitches according to the pattern, p4 (29, 29, 34 stitches).

Row 6 (decrease): sl1, k3, work next 23 (23, 28) stitches according to the pattern, sl1, k1, psso (28, 28, 33 stitches).

Row 7: sl1, work next 23 (23, 28) stitches according to the pattern, p4.

Row 8 (decrease): sl1, k3, work next 22 (22, 27) stitches according to the pattern, sl1, k1, psso (27, 27, 32 stitches).

Row 9: sl1, work next 22 (22, 27) stitches according to the pattern, p4.

Row 10 (decrease): sl1, k3, work next 21 (21, 26) stitches according to the pattern, sl1, k1, psso (26, 26, 31 stitches).

Row 11: sl1, work next 21 (21, 26) stitches according to the pattern, p4.

Row 12 (decrease): sl1, k3, work next 20 (20, 25) stitches according to the pattern, sl1, k1, psso (25, 25, 30 stitches).

Row 13: sl1, work next 20 (20, 25) stitches according to the pattern, p4.

Stop decreasing at armhole for medium size, continuing to decrease for small and large sizes:

Row 14 (decrease): sl1, k3, work next 19 (24) stitches according to the pattern, sl1, k1, psso (24, 29 stitches).

Row 15: sl1, work next 19 (24) stitches according to the pattern, p4.

Row 16 (decrease): sl1, k3, work next 18 (23) stitches according to the pattern, sl1, k1, psso (23, 28 stitches).

Row 17: sl1, work next 18 (23) stitches according to the pattern, p4.

Row 18 (decrease): sl1, k3, work next 17 (22) stitches according to the pattern, sl1, k1, psso (22, 27 stitches).

Row 19: sl1, work next 17 (22) stitches according to the pattern, p4.

Row 20 (decrease): sl1, k3, work next 16 (21) stitches according to the pattern, sl1, k1, psso (21, 26 stitches).

Row 21: sl1, work next 16 (21) stitches according to the pattern, p4.

Row 22 (decrease): sl1, k3, work next 15 (20) stitches according to the pattern, sl1, k1, psso (20, 25 stitches).

Row 23: sl1, work next 15 (20) stitches according to the pattern, p4.

Stop decreasing for small and large sizes.

For all sizes, continue without decreasing but keep the pattern correct until your work measures 27 (28½, 30) in (68.5, 72.5, 76 cm) from cast-on edge, ending with a purl row.

Slip the remaining 20 (25, 25) stitches onto a stitch holder.

Rejoin yarn to the 34 (34, 39) stitches of the left front and start with a wrong side row:

Continue decreasing at armhole edge every row for 6 rows, then every alternate row.

Row 1 (decrease): sl1, p3, work next 28 (28, 33) stitches according to the pattern, p2tog (33, 33, 38 stitches).

Row 2 (decrease): sl1, k1, psso, work next 27 (27, 32) stitches according to the pattern, k4 (32, 32, 37 stitches).

Row 3 (decrease): sl1, p3, work next 26 (26, 31) stitches according to the pattern, p2tog (31, 31, 36 stitches).

Row 4 (decrease): sl1, k1, psso, work next 25 (25, 30) stitches according to the pattern, k4 (30, 30, 35 stitches).

Row 5 (decrease): sl1, p3, work next 24 (24, 29) stitches according to the pattern, p2tog (29, 29, 34 stitches).

Row 6 (decrease): sl1, k1, psso, work next 23 (23, 28) stitches according to the pattern, k4 (28, 28, 33 stitches).

Row 7: sl1, p3, work next 24 (24, 29) stitches according to the pattern.

Row 8 (decrease): sl1, k1, psso, work next 22 (22, 27) stitches according to the pattern, k4 (27, 27, 32 stitches).

Row 9: sl1, p3, work next 23 (23, 28) stitches according to the pattern.

Row 10 (decrease): sl1, k1, psso, work next 21 (21, 26) stitches according to the pattern, k4 (26, 26, 31 stitches).

Row 11: sl1, p3, work next 22 (22, 27) stitches according to the pattern.

Row 12 (decrease): sl1, k1, psso, work next 20 (20, 25) stitches according to the pattern, k4 (25, 25, 30 stitches).

Row 13: sl1, p3, work next 21 (21, 26) stitches according to the pattern.

Stop decreasing at armhole for medium size, continuing to decrease for small and large sizes:

Row 14 (decrease): sl1, k1, psso, work next 19 (24) stitches according to the pattern, k4 (24, 29 stitches).

Row 15: sl1, p3, work next 20 (25) stitches according to the pattern.

Row 16 (decrease): sl1, k1, psso, work next 18 (23) stitches according to the pattern, k4 (23, 28 stitches).

Row 17: sl1, p3, work next 19 (25) stitches according to the pattern.

Row 18 (decrease): sl1, k1, psso, work next 17 (22) stitches according to the pattern, k4 (22, 27 stitches).

Row 19: sl1, p3, work next 18 (23) stitches according to the pattern.

Row 20 (decrease): sl1, k1, psso, work next 16 (21) stitches according to the pattern, k4 (21, 26 stitches).

Row 21: sl1, p3, work next 17 (22) stitches according to the pattern.

Row 22 (decrease): sl1, k1, psso, work next 15 (20) stitches according to the pattern, k4 (20, 25 stitches).

Row 23: sl1, p3, work next 16 (21) stitches according to the pattern.

Stop decreasing for small and large sizes:

For all sizes, continue without decreasing and keeping the pattern correct until work measures 27 (28½, 30) in (68.5, 72.5, 76.25 cm) from cast-on edge, ending with a purl row.

Slip the remaining 20 (25, 25) stitches onto a stitch holder.

To make shoulder seams:

Slip the stitches for the front and back onto 2 needles. With the right sides of the front and back together, hold the needles side by side and, using a third needle, pick up and knit one stitch together from each needle. At the same time, loosely bind off 20 (25, 25) stitches knitwise from each needle to form the shoulder seam. If you prefer, you can bind off each and then sew them together, but I prefer this technique as it provides a lovely even seam.

To make the neck/collar, using a US 7 (4.5 mm) circular needle, pick up stitches evenly around the neck:

Pick up and knit 16 stitches across the back, 101 (109, 117) along the left front edge, 2 at the front divide and 101 (109, 117) along the right front edge (220, 236, 252).

Round 1 (decrease): (k2, p2) for the first 112 (122, 128) stitches, k2, p1, k2tog, sl1, k1, psso, p1, (k2, p2) to the end of the round (218, 234, 250 stitches).

Note: the following stitches — k2tog, sl1, k1, psso — form the center of the V shape.

Round 2 (decrease): (k2, p2) for the first 112 (122, 128) stitches, k2, k2tog, sl1, k1, psso, (k2, p2) to the end of the round (216, 232, 248 stitches).

Round 3 (decrease): (k2, p2) for the first 112 (122, 128) stitches, k1, k2tog, sl1, k1, psso, k1, p2, (k2, p2) to the end of the round (214, 230, 246 stitches).

Round 4 (decrease): (k2, p2) for the first 112 (122, 128) stitches, k2tog, sl1, k1, psso, p2, (k2, p2) to the end of the round (212, 228, 244 stitches).

Round 5 (decrease): (k2, p2) for the first 108 (118, 124) stitches, k2, p1, k2tog, sl1, k1, psso, p1, (k2, p2) to the end of the round (210, 226, 242 stitches).

Round 6 (decrease): (k2, p2) for the first 108 (118, 124) stitches, k2, k2tog, sl1, k1, psso, (k2, p2) to the end of the round (208, 224, 240 stitches).

Round 7 (decrease): (k2, p2) for the first 108 (118, 124) stitches, k1, k2tog, sl1, k1, psso, k1, p2, (k2, p2) to the end of the round (206, 222, 238 stitches).

Round 8 (decrease): (k2, p2) for the first 108 (118, 124) stitches, k2tog, sl1, k1, psso, p2, (k2, p2) to the end of the round (204, 220, 236 stitches).

Round 9 (decrease): (k2, p2) for the first 104 (114, 120) stitches, k2, p1, k2tog, sl1, k1, psso, p1, (k2, p2) to the end of the round (202, 218, 234 stitches).

Round 10 (decrease): (k2, p2) for the first 104 (114, 120) stitches, k2, k2tog, sl1, k1, psso, (k2, p2) to the end of the round (200, 216, 232 stitches).

Round 11 (decrease): (k2, p2) for the first 104 (114, 120) stitches, k1, k2tog, sl1, k1, psso, k1, p2, (k2, p2) to the end of the round (198, 214, 230 stitches).

Round 12 (decrease): (k2, p2) for the first 104 (114, 120) stitches, k2tog, sl1, k1, psso, p2, (k2, p2) to the end of the round (196, 212, 228 stitches).

Round 13 (decrease): (k2, p2) for the first 100 (110, 116) stitches, k2, p1, k2tog, sl1, k1, psso, p1, (k2, p2) to the end of the round (194, 210, 226 stitches.

Round 14 (decrease): (k2, p2) for the first 100 (110, 116) stitches, k1, k2tog, sl1, k1, psso, (k2, p2) to the end of the round (192, 208, 224 stitches.

Round 15 (decrease): (k2, p2) for the first 100 (110, 116) stitches, k2tog, sl1, k1, psso, p2, (k2, p2) to the end of the round (190, 206, 222 stitches.

Round 16: Bind off loosely keeping k2, p2 pattern correct.

To finish the armholes, starting at the middle of the armhole, pick up 124 (140, 156) stitches evenly around the armhole using a US 5 (3.75 mm) circular needle:

Round 1: (k2, p2) repeat to the end of the round.

Round 2: (p2, k2) repeat to the end of the round.

Round 3 (decrease): sl1, k1, psso, (k2, p2) to last

5 stitches, k2, p1, k2tog (122, 138, 154 stitches).

Round 4 (decrease): sl1, k1, psso, k1, p2, (k2, p2) to last 4 stitches, k2, k2tog (120, 136, 152 stitches).

Round 5 (decrease): sl1, k1, psso, p2, (k2, p2) to last 3 stitches, k1, k2tog (118, 134, 150 stitches).

Round 6 (decrease): sl1, k1, psso, p1, (k2, p2) to last 2 stitches, k2tog (116, 132, 148 stitches).

Round 7 (decrease): sl1, k1, psso, (k2, p2) to last 5 stitches, k2, p1, k2tog (114, 130, 146 stitches).

Round 8 (decrease): sl1, k1, psso, k1, p2, (k2, p2) to last 4 stitches, k2, k2tog (112, 128, 144 stitches).

Round 9 (decrease): sl1, k1, psso, p2, (k2, p2) to last 3 stitches, k1, k2tog (110, 126, 142 stitches).

Round 10: (decrease): sl1, k1, psso, p2, (k2, p2) to last 2 stitches, k2tog (108, 124, 140 stitches).

Round 11: Bind off loosely keeping k2, p2 pattern correct.

Repeat for other armhole.

TO FINISH

Break off yarn leaving an 8 in (20 cm) tail and tie off securely. Using a darning needle, weave yarn tails into stitches on the wrong side.

CABLED BEANIE

Knitted in the round | Level: Intermediate

FINISHED MEASUREMENTS:

This one-size hat will fit head circumference from 20–23 in (50.75–58.5 cm). It is slightly stretchy.

YARN:

The Rare Yarns Company Tree Children

80% alpaca, 20% merino; 1.76 oz (50 g) skein; 110 yds (100.5 m)

Main Color (MC) 2 skeins: shade TW843 Blue Days

NEEDLES:

US 5 (3.75 mm) 12 in (30 cm) circular needle and/or set of double-pointed needles and a cable needle

GAUGE:

US 5 (3.75 mm) needles, 20 stitches x 26 rows = 4 in (10 cm) over k2, p2 rib pattern. Adjust the needle size as needed to get the correct tension.

This classic cabled hat is delightfully cozy. The design incorporates an oversized, folded up brim which, although very deep, clings securely yet softly to your head. The simple cable pattern has been designed to resemble a twisted boat rope. It's a hat that would look good on the ski field, as well as on an early morning fishing expedition. I have used a very soft alpaca/merino blend for mine and I really think this is a hat that is best knitted in a single color, or subtle tweed yarn, to highlight the cable pattern.

Cast on 120 stitches loosely using US 5 (3.75 mm) circular needle or double-pointed needles.

Do not turn the needles at the end of the round, just keep going in the same direction, working on right side of work. Place marker, if using, and slip on every round.

Work 5 in (12.75 cm) in k2, p2 rib pattern.

Start cable pattern:

Round 1: *k8, p4*, repeat from *to* to the end of the round.

Round 2 (cable round): *sl4 stitches onto cn, hold at front, k4 from left-hand needle, k4 from cn, p4*, repeat from *to* to the end of the round.

Rounds 3–7: *k8, p4*, repeat from *to* to the end of the round.

Repeat rounds 2–7, 4 more times.

Your work should measure 9 in (22.75 cm) from the cast-on row.

Start to decrease for the crown:

Round 32: (cable round): *sl4 stitches onto cn, hold at front, k4 from left-hand needle, k4 from cn, p4*, repeat from *to* to the end of the round.

Round 33 (decrease): *k8, p2tog, p2*, repeat from *to* to the end of the round (110 stitches).

Rounds 34–37: *k8, p3*, repeat from *to* to the end of the round.

Round 38 (cable round): *sl4 stitches onto cn, hold at front, k4 from left-hand needle, k4 from cn, p3*, repeat from *to* to the end of the round.

Round 39 (decrease): *k8, p1, p2tog*, repeat from *to* to the end of the round (100 stitches).

Rounds 40–43: *k8, p2*, repeat from *to* to the end of the round.

Round 44 (cable round) (decrease): *sl4 stitches onto cn, hold at front, k2tog, k2 from left-hand needle, k2tog, k2 from cn, p2*, repeat from *to* to the end of the round (80 stitches).

Rounds 45–46: *k6, p2*, repeat from *to* to the end of the round.

Change to double-pointed needles if using a circular needle:

Round 47 (decrease): *k6, p2tog*, repeat from *to* to the end of the round (70 stitches).

Rounds 48–49: *k6, p1*, repeat from *to* to the end of the round.

Round 50 (cable round): *sl3 stitches onto cn, hold at front, k2tog, k1 from left-hand needle, k2tog, k1 from cn, p1*, repeat from *to* to the end of the round (50 stitches).

Rounds 51–55: *k4, p1*, repeat from *to* to the end of the round.

Round 56 (cable round): *sl2 stitches onto cn, hold at front, k2tog from left-hand needle, k2tog from cn, p1*, repeat from *to* to the end of the round (30 stitches).

Round 57 (decrease): *k2tog, p1*, repeat from *to* to the end of the round (20 stitches).

Round 58 (decrease): k2tog, repeat to the end of the round (10 stitches).

Break off yarn leaving an 8 in (20 cm) tail. Draw tail through remaining stitches and pull tight, feed through to wrong side and tie off.

TO FINISH

Using a darning needle, weave yarn tail into stitches on the wrong side.

NATURE'S STRIPES SCARF

Knitted flat   Level: Easy

This very simple scarf uses three colors worked in stocking stitch and reverse stocking stitch stripes. It is not worked lengthways, but instead you knit across the scarf, starting at one long edge using a long circular needle to hold all of the stitches. You use the circular needle as if using straight needles, turning at the end of each row. I have intentionally used a larger needle than recommended for the yarn weight to give the scarf a softer feel and I have chosen colors that remind me of the ocean.

FINISHED MEASUREMENTS:

The scarf is 60 in (152.5 cm) in length and 7 in (17.75 cm) wide. You can increase the length by adding extra stitches — for every 4 in (10 cm) increase or decrease in length, add or subtract 10 stitches.

YARN:

Zealana Kauri

60% merino, 30% brushtail possum, 10% mulberry silk; 1.76 oz (50 g) skein; 94 yds (86 m)

Contrast Color (CC1)
1 skein: shade Blue Awa K15

Contrast Color (CC2)
1 skein: shade K05 Punga Fern

Contrast Color (CC3)
1 skein: shade K13 Ashen

NEEDLES:

US 10½ (6.5 mm) circular needle, at least 24 in (60 cm) in length

GAUGE:

US 10½ (6.5 mm) needles, 10 stitches x 11 rows = 4 in (10 cm) over pattern. Adjust the needle size as needed to get the correct tension.

To start the scarf, using CC 1 (dark blue), cast on 136 stitches with a US 10½ (6.5 mm) circular needle:

Row 1: knit (remember to turn and work as for straight needles).

Work 4 rows of stocking stitch (one row purl, one row knit).

Row 6: Change to CC2 (turquoise), knit.

Work 4 rows of stocking stitch (one row purl, one row knit).

Row 11: Change to CC3 (grey), purl.

Work 4 rows of stocking stitch (one row knit, one row purl).

Row 16: Change to CC2, knit.

Work 4 rows of stocking stitch (one row purl, one row knit).

Row 21: Change to CC3, purl.

Work 4 rows of stocking stitch (one row knit, one row purl).

Row 26: Change to CC2, knit.

Work 4 rows of stocking stitch (one row purl, one row knit).

Row 31: Change to CC1, purl.

Work 4 rows of stocking stitch (one row knit, one row purl).
Bind off loosely knitwise.

Sew in loose yarn tails along the short edges.

To finish the scarf ends, using CC1, pick and knit 28 stitches along the edge:

Row 1: purl.

Row 2: knit.

Row 3: purl.

Row 4: knit.

Row 5: purl.

Bind off loosely knitwise. Roll this finished edge and sew into place on the wrong side. This should cover up the ends of the rows where you changed yarn colors. Repeat for the other end.

TO FINISH

Break off yarn leaving an 8 in (20 cm) tail and tie off securely. Using a darning needle, weave yarn tails into stitches on the wrong side.

Knitted in the round and flat   Level: Intermediate

FINISHED MEASUREMENTS:

Small: 40 in (101.5 cm) chest, 24 in (60 cm) length (from shoulder)

Medium: 44 in (111.75 cm) chest, 26 in (66 cm) length (from shoulder)

Large: 48 in (122 cm) chest, 28 in (71 cm) length (from shoulder)

Note: The length is easily adjusted — see instructions

YARN:

Touch Yarns Hand-Dyed Possum Merino DK

60% merino, 30% possum, 10% silk; 3.5 oz (100 g) skein; 460 yds (420.5 m)

2 (2, 3) skeins: shade C12

NEEDLES:

US 5 (3.75 mm) straight needles and set of US 5 (3.75 mm) double-pointed needles or 14 in (35.5 cm) circular needle

GAUGE:

Using US 5 (3.75 mm) needles, 22 stitches x 26 rows = 4 in (10 cm) over yoke pattern. Adjust the needle size as needed to get the correct tension.

This simple pattern features a hand-painted yarn and stitch work to create the texture. It's very lightweight, yet warm, and the kind of vest that you could wear over a T-shirt on a cooler spring day, or over a woolen turtleneck in the middle of winter. It is worked from the neck down: you start with the yoke, knitting across and work downwards for the main body of the vest, eventually ending at the bottom edge. To maintain a completely random appearance with this yarn (or any variegated yarn) it's best that you work with two balls of wool and alternate rows between the two as I have with this garment.

To start the yoke, cast on 69 (73, 77) stitches with US 5 (3.75 mm) straight needles:

Row 1: *k1tbl, p1*, repeat from *to* to the last stitch, k1.

Row 2: p1, *k1tbl, p1*, repeat from *to* to the end.

Repeat rows 1 and 2 until work measures 4 (4½, 5) in (10, 11.5, 12.75 cm) from the cast-on edge.

Divide for neck opening:

Slip first 32 stitches onto a stitch holder, continue to work in the rib pattern above on remaining 37 (41, 45) stitches until work measures 8 (9, 10) in (20.25, 22.75, 25.5 cm) from the cast-on edge. Place these stitches onto a second stitch holder.

Return to the 32 stitches on the first holder, with right side facing:

Row 1 (decrease): *k1tbl, p1*, repeat from *to* to the last 2 stitches, k2tog.

Row 2: p1, *k1tbl, p1*, repeat from *to* to the end.

Decrease every alternate row, keeping the rib pattern correct, until you have 2 stitches remaining, k2tog and tie off.

To complete the other side of the yoke, cast on 69 (73, 77) stitches with US 5 (3.75 mm) straight needles:

Row 1: *k1tbl, p1*, repeat from *to* to the last stitch, k1.

Row 2: p1,*k1tbl, p1*, repeat from *to* to the end.

Repeat rows 1 & 2 until work measures 4 (4½, 5) in (10, 11.5, 12.75 cm).

Divide for neck opening:

Work the first 37 (41, 45) stitches in the rib pattern and slip the last 32 stitches onto a stitch holder and continue to work on the remaining 37 (41, 45) stitches until work measures 8 (9, 10) in (20, 22.75, 25.5 cm) from the cast-on edge. Place these stitches onto a second stitch holder.

Return to the 32 stitches on the first holder, with right side facing:

Row 1 (decrease): sl1, k1tbl, psso, *p1, k1tbl*, repeat from *to* to the end of the row.

Row 2: p1, *k1tbl, p1*, repeat from *to* to the end.

Decrease every alternate row, keeping the rib pattern correct, until you have 2 stitches remaining, k2tog and tie off.

To join the two sides of the yoke at the back:

Place the stitches on the holders back onto 2 needles (one for each side). With the right sides together, hold the needles side by side and, using a third needle, pick up and knit one stitch from each needle together and at the same time, bind off loosely knitwise.

To start the main body:

First you are going to make the small overlap at the front neck (see photo opposite).

Lay the yoke flat, with the right side facing up. Lay the two shaped forward pieces so that the longer straight edges lie parallel and the lower edge of each overlap slightly.

Place the left-hand one on top of the right-hand one. You may want to pin this in place or weave a loose yarn through the two front sections to keep them in place while you do the next step.

Front and back body sections (both are the same):

With right side facing, pick up and knit 121 (129, 137) stitches evenly across the bottom edge of the yoke. You will need to work through the two layers at the front.

Row 1: *k1, p3*, repeat from *to* to the last stitch, k1.

Row 2: *p1, k3*, repeat from *to* to the last stitch, p1.

Repeat until work measures 3 (3½, 4) in (7.5, 8.75, 10 cm) from where you joined the yoke, ending with row 1.

Start armhole shaping:

Row 1: purl.

Row 2: purl.

Row 3 (increase): kfb, knit to last stitch, kfb (123, 131, 139 stitches).

Repeat these last 3 rows 5 more times (133, 141, 149 stitches).

Stop increasing and continue, keeping pattern correct (purl 2 rows, knit 1 row), until your work measures 7 (8, 9) in (17.75, 20, 22.75 cm) from where you joined the yoke, ending with a wrong side row.

Purl 1 row.

Complete bottom rib section:

Note: You can adjust the length at this point to any desired length. The given lengths are a guide only.

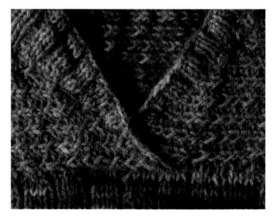

Row 1: p1, *k1tbl, p1*, repeat from *to* to the end.

Row 2: *k1tbl, p1*, repeat from *to* to the last stitch, k1tbl.

Repeat rows 1 & 2 until work measures 15 (17, 19) in (38, 43, 48.25 cm) from where you joined the yoke. Bind off loosely in rib pattern.

With right sides of the front and back together, sew the side seams.

To add armhole edgings, with right side facing, start at the side seam using US 5 (3.75 mm) double-pointed needles or circular needle to pick up and knit 138 (150, 162) stitches evenly around the armhole edge:

Round 1: *k2, p2*, repeat from *to* to the last 2 stitches, k2.

Round 2 (decrease): k2tog, p2, *k2, p2*, repeat from *to* to the last 2 stitches, sl1, k1, psso (136, 148, 160 stitches).

Round 3 (decrease): k2tog, p1, *k2, p2*, repeat from *to* to the last 5 stitches, k2, p1, sl1, k1, psso (134, 146, 158 stitches).

Round 4 (decrease): k2tog, *k2, p2*, repeat from *to* to the last 4 stitches, k2, sl1, k1, psso (132, 144, 156 stitches).

Round 5 (decrease): k2tog, k1, p2, *k2, p2*, repeat from *to* to the last 3 stitches, k1, sl1, k1, psso (130, 142, 154 stitches).

Round 6 (decrease): k2tog, p2, *k2, p2*, repeat from *to* to the last 2 stitches, sl1, k1, psso (128, 140, 152 stitches).

Round 7 (decrease): k2tog, p1 *k2, p2*, repeat from *to* to the last 5 stitches, k2, p1, sl1, k1, psso (126, 138, 150 stitches).

Round 8 (decrease): k2tog, *k2, p2*, repeat from *to* to the last 4 stitches, k2, sl1, k1, psso (124, 136, 148) stitches)

Round 9 (decrease): k2tog, k1, p2, *k2, p2*, repeat from *to* to the last 3 stitches, k1, sl1, k1, psso (122, 134, 146 stitches).

Round 10 (decrease): k2tog, p2, *k2, p2*, repeat from *to* to the last 2 stitches, sl1, k1, psso (120, 132, 144 stitches).

Round 11 (decrease): k2tog, p1 *k2, p2*, repeat from *to* to the last 5 stitches, k2, p1, sl1, k1, psso (118, 130, 142 stitches).

Bind off loosely in rib pattern.

Repeat for other armhole.

To complete neck edging, with right side facing, using US 5 (3.75 mm) straight needles or circular needle, pick up and knit 40 (52, 64) stitches evenly across the back neck edge:

Row 1: *k2, p2*, repeat from *to* to the end, turn.

Row 2 (increase): *k2, p2*, repeat from *to* to the end, then pick up 6 stitches and incorporate them into the pattern, turn (46, 58, 70 stitches).

Row 3 (increase): *p2, k2*, repeat from *to* to the end, then pick up 6 stitches and incorporate them into the pattern, turn (52, 64, 76 stitches.)

Row 4 (increase): *k2, p2*, repeat from *to* to the end, then pick up 6 stitches and incorporate them into the pattern, turn (58, 70, 82 stitches).

Row 5 (increase): *p2, k2*, repeat from *to* to the end, then pick up 6 stitches and incorporate them into the pattern, turn (64, 76, 88 stitches).

Row 6 (increase): *k2, p2*, repeat from *to* to the end, then pick up 6 stitches and incorporate them into the pattern, turn (70, 82, 94 stitches).

Row 7 (increase): *p2, k2*, repeat from *to* to the end, then pick up 6 stitches and incorporate them into the pattern, turn (76, 88, 100 stitches).

Row 8 (increase): *k2, p2*, repeat from *to* to the end, then pick up 6 stitches and incorporate them into the pattern, turn (82, 94, 106 stitches).

Row 9 (increase): *p2, k2*, repeat from *to* to the end, then pick up 6 stitches and incorporate them into the pattern, turn (88, 100, 112 stitches).

Row 10 (increase): *k2, p2*, repeat from *to* to the end, then pick up 6 stitches and incorporate them into the pattern, turn (94, 106, 118 stitches).

Row 11 (increase): *p2, k2*, repeat from *to* to the end, then pick up 6 stitches and incorporate them into the pattern, turn (100, 112, 124 stitches).

Row 12 (increase): *k2, p2*, repeat from *to* to the end, then pick up 6 stitches and incorporate them into the pattern, turn (106, 118, 130 stitches).

Row 13 (increase): *p2, k2*, repeat from *to* to the end, then pick up 6 stitches and incorporate them into the pattern, turn (112, 124, 136 stitches).

Row 14 (increase): *k2, p2*, repeat from *to* to the end, then pick up 6 stitches and incorporate them into the pattern, turn (118, 130, 142 stitches).

Row 15 (increase): *p2, k2*, repeat from *to* to the end, then pick up 6 stitches and incorporate them into the pattern, turn (124, 136, 148 stitches).

Row 16 (increase): *k2, p2*, repeat from *to* to the end, then pick up 6 stitches and incorporate them into the pattern, turn (130, 142, 154 stitches).

Row 17 (increase): *p2, k2*, repeat from *to* to the end, then pick up 6 stitches and incorporate them into the pattern, turn (136, 148, 160 stitches).

Row 18 (increase): *k2, p2*, repeat from *to* to the end, then pick up 6 stitches and incorporate them into the pattern, turn (142, 154, 166 stitches).

Row 19 (increase): *p2, k2*, repeat from *to* to the end, then pick up 6 stitches and incorporate them into the pattern, turn (148, 160, 172 stitches).

Row 20 (increase): *k2, p2*, repeat from *to* to the end, then pick up 6 stitches and incorporate them into the pattern, turn (154, 166, 178 stitches).

You should now have picked up stitches across the entire neck opening. If you have not yet reached the end of the crossover section at the front, then continue to increase in order to complete the entire neck edge. Once you have all of the stitches picked up, then bind off loosely in the k2, p2 rib pattern.

TO FINISH

Make sure ends of yarn are tied off securely and weave in yarn tails in wrong side.

SLEEVELESS HOODIE

Knitted in the round   Level: Intermediate

This is an essential piece for anyone who spends time outside. A sleeveless hoodie will keep your body and head warm, leaving your arms free for your activity, and the pocket or muff at the front is perfect for warming your hands in between. I have used a deep sea blue for my hoodie — there is a subtle wide rib that continues up the front from the pocket to the hood. This rib pattern is repeated at each side, adding interest to what is really a rather plain tube of stocking stitch.

FINISHED MEASUREMENTS:

Small: 42 in (106.5 cm) chest, 29 in (73.5 cm) length (from shoulder), shoulder width (neck to armhole) 5 in (12.75 cm)

Medium: 45½ in (115.5 cm) chest, 31 in (78.75 cm) length (from shoulder), shoulder width (neck to armhole) 6 in (15.25 cm)

Large: 49 in (124.5 cm) chest, 33 in (84 cm) length (from shoulder), shoulder width (neck to armhole) 7 in (17.75 cm)

YARN:

Zealana Kauri 10 ply

60% merino, 30% brushtail possum, 10% mulberry silk; 1.76 oz (50 g) skein; 94 yds (86 m)

10 (12, 14) skeins: shade Blue Awa K15

NEEDLES:

US 5 (3.75 mm) and US 7 (4.5 mm) 24 in (60 cm) circular needles, two US 7 (4.5 mm) straight needles and US 5 (3.75 mm) double-pointed needles for the I-cord, plus several stitch holders

GAUGE:

Using US 7 (4.5 mm) needles, 14 stitches x 20 rows = 4 in (10 cm) over stocking stitch. Adjust the needle size as needed to get the correct tension.

Cast on 144 (156, 168) stitches using US 5 (3.75 mm) circular needle and start working in the round:

Place marker, if using, and slip on every round. Do not turn the needles at the end of the round, just keep going in the same direction, working on the right side of work.

Work k2, p1 rib for 3 in (7.5 cm).

Change to US 7 (4.5 mm) circular needle:

Round 1 (increase): (k2, p1) twice, k11, kfb next 37 (43, 49) stitches, k11, (p1, k2) 4 times, p1, k59 (65, 71), p1, (k2, p1) twice (181, 199, 217 stitches).

Round 2: (k2, p1) twice, k11, (k1, sl1 onto holder and hold at front) 37 (43, 49) times, k11, (p1, k2) 4 times, p1, k59 (65, 71), p1, (k2, p1) twice (144, 156, 168 stitches).

You should now have 37 (43, 49) stitches on the holder, which will be the foundation row of the muff/pocket at the front.

Round 3: (k2, p1) twice, k59 (65, 71), (p1, k2) 4 times, p1, k59 (65, 71), p1, (k2, p1) twice.

Repeat this row until work measures 10 (11, 12) in (25.5, 28, 30.5 cm) from the cast-on edge.

To complete the muff or pocket, using straight needles, work on the 37 (43, 49) stitches on the holder:

Pocket row 1: p1, *k2, p1*, repeat from *to* to the end, turn.

Pocket row 2: k1, *p2, k1*, repeat from *to* to the end, turn.

Repeat these two rows until work measures 3 in (7.5 cm) from

the start of the flap, ending with a pocket row 2 and start decreasing to shape the top.

Pocket row 3 (decrease): sl1, k1, psso, k1, *p1, k2*, repeat from *to* to the last 3 stitches, k1, k2tog, turn (35, 41, 47 stitches).

Pocket row 4: *p2, k1*, repeat from *to* to the end, turn.

Pocket row 5 (decrease): sl1, k1, psso, *p1, k2*, repeat from *to* to the last 2 stitches, k2tog, turn (33, 39, 45 stitches).

Pocket row 6: p1, *k1, p2*, repeat from *to* to the last stitch, p1, turn.

Pocket row 7: (decrease): sl1, k1, psso, *k2, p1*, repeat from *to* to last 2 stitches, p2tog (31, 37, 43 stitches).

Repeat rows 2–7 until there are 19 (25, 31) stitches remaining.

Work straight keeping pattern correct until the pocket flap measures 7 (8, 9) in (17.75, 20, 22.75 cm).

To continue with the main body:

The next row will join the pocket flap and main body together. Return to your work on the circular needle.

Joining row: (k2, p1) twice, k20, (k1 from each needle at the same time) 19 (25, 31) times, k20, (p1, k2) 4 times, p1, k59 (65, 71), p1, (k2, p1) twice (144, 156, 168 stitches).

Next row: (k2, p1) twice, k23, (p1, k2) 4 (6, 8) times, p1, k23, (p1, k2) 4 times, p1, k59 (65, 71), p1, (k2, p1) twice.

Repeat last row until work measures 20 (22, 23) in (50.75, 55.75, 58.5 cm) from the cast-on edge.

To create armholes:

Next row: (k2, p1) twice, k23, (p1, k2) 4 (6, 8) times, p1, k23, p1, k2, p1, bind off 5 stitches, p1, k2, p1, k59 (65, 71), p1, k2, p1, bind off 3 stitches (136, 148, 160 stitches).

Work on back section only:

Rejoin yarn to back with right side facing.

Back row 1: sl1, k2, p1, p59 (65, 71), p1, k2, p1, turn (67, 73, 79 stitches).

Back row 2: sl1, p2, k1, k59 (65, 71), k1, p2, k1, turn.

Repeat back rows 1 and 2 until work measures 29 (31, 33) in (73.5, 78.75, 84 cm).

Place first 18 (21, 24) stitches onto a stitch holder, next 31 stitches onto a separate stitch holder and remaining 18 (21, 24) stitches onto a third holder. You can leave them on a needle if you don't have enough stitch holders.

Work on front section only:

Front row 1: bind off 2 stitches, k2, p1, k23, (p1, k2) 4 (6, 8) times, p1, k23, p1, k2, p1, turn (67, 73, 79 stitches).

Front row 2: sl1, p2, k1, p23, (k1, p2) 4 (6, 8) times, k1, p23, k1, p2, k1, turn.

Front row 3: sl1, k2, p1, k23, (p1, k2) 4 (6, 8) times, p1, k23 p1, k2, p1, turn.

Repeat front rows 2 & 3 until work measures 23 (25, 27) in (58.5, 63.5, 66 cm) ending with a front row 2.

Divide for neck:

Next row: sl1, k2, p1, k23, (p1, k2) 2 (3, 4) times, bind off 1 stitch, k1, p1, (k2, p1) 2 (3, 4) times, k24, p1, k2, p1, turn (66, 72, 78 stitches).

Keep working on the 33 (36, 39) stitches of the right side of front only:

Right front row 1: sl1, p2, k1, p23, (k1, p2) 2 (3, 4) times, turn.

Right front row 2: k2tog, yo, p1, (k2, p1) 1 (2, 3) times, k23, p1, k2, p1, turn.

Right front row 3: sl1, p2, k1, p23, (k1, p2) 2 (3, 4) times, turn.

Right front row 4: k2, p1, (k2, p1) 1 (2, 3) times, k23, p1, k2, p1, turn.

Repeat rows 3 & 4 once more.

Right front row 7: sl1, p2, k1, p23, (k1, p2) 2 (3, 4) times, turn.

Right front row 8: k2tog, yo, p1, (k2, p1) 1 (2, 3) times, k23, p1, k2, p1, turn.

Repeat rows 3–8, 3 times. Do not bind off.

Place first 15 stitches onto a stitch holder and

the remaining 18 (21, 24) stitches onto another stitch holder.

Rejoin yarn with wrong side facing and work on the 33 (36, 39) stitches of the left side of front only:

Left front row 1: (k1, p2) 2 (3, 4) times, k1, p23, k1, p2, k1, turn.

Left front row 2: sl1, k2, p1, k23, (p1, k2) 1 (2, 3) times, p1, yo, k2tog, turn.

Left front row 3: (k1, p2) 2 (3, 4) times, k1, p23, k1, p2, k1 turn.

Left front row 4: sl1, k2, p1, k23, (p1, k2) 2 (3, 4) times, turn.

Repeat rows 3 & 4 once more.

Left front row 7: (k1, p2) 2 (3, 4) times, p1, p23, k1, p2, k1, turn.

Left front row 8: sl1, k2, p1, k24, (p1, k2) 1 (2, 3) times, p1, yo, k2tog, turn.

Repeat rows 3–8, 3 times. Do not bind off.

Place first 15 stitches onto a holder and the remaining 18 (21, 24) stitches onto another stitch holder.

To make shoulder seams:

Place the 18 (21, 24) stitches from the right front and right back onto 2 needles (1 for each side). With the right sides together, hold the needles side by side and, using a third needle, pick up and knit 1 stitch from each needle together, and at the same time bind off loosely knitwise. Repeat for the left shoulder.

To make the hood, place all remaining stitches onto the circular needle:

With right side facing, start with the 15 stitches from the left side, then the 31 stitches from the back, then the 15 stitches from the right side (61 stitches).

Hood row 1 (increase): (k2, p1) twice, k5, kfb 39 times, k5, (p1, k2) twice, turn (100 stitches).

Hood row 2: (p2, k1) twice, p88 (k1, p2) twice, turn.

Hood row 3: knit.

Hood row 4: (k2, p1) twice, p88, (p1, k2) twice, turn.

Repeat rows 3 & 4 until hood measures 5 (6, 7) in (12.75, 15.25, 17.75 cm) ending with a wrong side row (hood row 4).

Start to shape the hood by decreasing on the next and every alternate row:

Hood row 5 (decrease): (k2, p1) twice, k42, sl1, k2tog, psso, k43, (p1, k2) twice, turn (98 stitches).

Hood row 6: (p2, k1) twice, p86, (k1, p2) twice, turn.

Hood row 7 (decrease): (k2, p1) twice, k41, sl1, k2tog, psso, k42, (p1, k2) twice, turn (96 stitches).

Hood row 8: (p2, k1) twice, p84, (k1, p2) twice, turn.

Hood row 9 (decrease): (k2, p1) twice, k40, sl1, k2tog, psso, k41, (p1, k2) twice, turn (94 stitches).

Hood row 10: (p2, k1) twice, p82, (k1, p2) twice, turn.

Hood row 11 (decrease): (k2, p1) twice, k39, sl1, k2tog, psso, k40, (p1, k2) twice, turn (92 stitches).

Hood row 12: (p2, k1) twice, p80, (k1, p2) twice, turn.

Hood row 13 (decrease): (k2, p1) twice, k38, sl1, k2tog, psso, k39, (p1, k2) twice, turn (90 stitches).

Hood row 14: (p2, k1) twice, p78, (k1, p2) twice, turn.

Hood row 15 (decrease): (k2, p1) twice, k37, sl1, k2tog, psso, k38, (p1, k2) twice, turn (88 stitches).

Hood row 16: (p2, k1) twice, p76, (k1, p2) twice, turn.

Hood row 17 (decrease): (k2, p1) twice, k36, sl1, k2tog, psso, k37, (p1, k2) twice, turn (86 stitches).

Hood row 18: (p2, k1) twice, p74, (k1, p2) twice, turn.

Hood row 19 (decrease): (k2, p1) twice, k35, sl1, k2tog, psso, k36, (p1, k2) twice, turn (84 stitches).

Hood row 20: (p2, k1) twice, p72, (k1, p2) twice, turn.

Hood row 21 (decrease): (k2, p1) twice, k34, sl1, k2tog, psso, k35, (p1, k2) twice, turn (82 stitches).

Hood row 22: (p2, k1) twice, p70, (k1, p2) twice, turn.

Hood row 23 (decrease): (k2, p1) twice, k33, sl1, k2tog, psso, k34, (p1, k2) twice, turn (80 stitches).

Hood row 24: (p2, k1) twice, p68, (k1, p2) twice, turn.

Hood row 25 (decrease): (k2, p1) twice, k32, sl1, k2tog, psso, k33, (p1, k2) twice, turn (78 stitches).

Hood row 26: (p2, k1) twice, p66, (k1, p2) twice, turn.

Hood row 27 (decrease): (k2, p1) twice, k31, sl1, k2tog, psso, k32, (p1, k2) twice, turn (76 stitches).

Hood row 28: (p2, k1) twice, p64, (k1, p2) twice, turn.

Hood row 29 (decrease): (k2, p1) twice, k30, sl1, k2tog, psso, k31, (p1, k2) twice, turn (74 stitches).

Hood row 30: (p2, k1) twice, p62, (k1, p2) twice, turn.

Hood row 31 (decrease): (k2, p1) twice, k29, sl1, k2tog, psso, k30, (p1, k2) twice, turn (72 stitches).

Hood row 32: (p2, k1) twice, p60, (k1, p2) twice, turn.

Hood row 33 (decrease): (k2, p1) twice, k28 sl1, k2tog, psso, k29, (p1, k2) twice, turn (70 stitches).

Hood row 34: (p2, k1) twice, p58, (k1, p2) twice, turn.

Hood row 35 (decrease): (k2, p1) twice, k27, sl1, k2tog, psso, k28, (p1, k2) twice, turn (68 stitches).

Hood row 36: (p2, k1) twice, p56, (k1, p2) twice, turn.

Hood row 37 (decrease): (k2, p1) twice, k26, sl1, k2tog, psso, k27, (p1, k2) twice, turn (66 stitches).

Hood row 38: (p2, k1) twice, p54, (k1, p2) twice, turn.

Hood row 39 (decrease): (k2, p1) twice, k25, sl1, k2tog, psso, k26, (p1, k2) twice, turn (64 stitches).

Hood row 40: (p2, k1) twice, p52, (k1, p2) twice, turn.

To finish, divide the stitches onto 2 needles — 32 stitches on each needle — with the hood edge at the top of the needle. With the right sides together, hold the needles side by side and, using a third needle, pick up and knit one stitch from each needle and at the same time bind off loosely knitwise. Tie off securely.

TO FINISH

Using the main color, make an I-cord that is 36 in (91.5 cm) long to thread through the holes at the front neck opening. To make I-cord, using the US 5 (3.75 mm) double-pointed needles cast on 4 stitches. Every row is a knit row worked without turning the needles. At the end of each row, without turning, push the stitches to the other end of the needle and pull the yarn tightly behind the stitches and start knitting from the opposite end from where you finished. Keep going until the required length is reached. Sew the side edges of the muff/pocket in place. Make sure ends of yarn are tied off securely and weave in yarn tails in wrong side.

LONG SCARF

Knitted flat   Level: Easy

This scarf is worked on big needles and features an easy cable pattern that you will master in no time. The yarn is an exquisite brushed blend of alpaca, mohair and, of course, merino. The result is a lovely soft, warm scarf that you will have finished in an evening.

FINISHED MEASUREMENTS:

The scarf is 75 in (190.5 cm) in length and 8 in (20 cm) wide

YARN:

Rare Yarns Company's Rare Fire Brushed 14 ply

50% alpaca, 30% mohair and 20% superfine merino; 1.76 oz (50 g) skein; 87 yards (79.5 m)

5 skeins: shade #400 Jewel Fire

NEEDLES:

US 10½ (6.5 mm) straight needles, plus a cable needle

GAUGE:

Using US 10½ (6.5 mm) needles, 12 stitches x 17 rows = 4 in (10 cm) over pattern. Adjust the needle size as needed to get the correct tension.

To start, cast on 24 stitches with US 10.5 (6.5 mm) straight needles.

Row 1: (k2, p2) twice, k8, (p2, k2) twice.

Row 2: (p2, k2) twice, p8, (k2, p2) twice.

Repeat rows 1 & 2, 7 more times.

Row 17 (cable row): (k2, p2) twice, sl2 onto cn, hold at front, k2, k2 from cn, sl2 onto cn, hold at back, k2, k2 from cn, (p2, k2) twice.

Row 18: (p2, k2) twice, p8, (k2, p2) twice.

Repeat rows 1 & 2, 7 more times.

These 32 rows form the pattern. Repeat them until your work measures 75 in (190.5 cm). Bind off loosely keeping pattern correct and ending with the row just before a cable.

The length can be adjusted as desired.

TO FINISH

Make sure ends of yarn are tied off securely and weave in yarn tail in wrong side.

SOURCING SUMPTUOUS MERINO YARNS

As I said in the introduction, this has been one of my most pleasurable craft experiences. Not only do these merino and merino blend yarns look great, they feel wonderful as well, and knitting with them has been a delightful process. I am grateful to the yarn companies listed on the following pages who supported this project: although some are located in Australia and New Zealand, they all sell their yarns overseas. All of the yarns were available at the time of printing, but if you want to substitute some, remember that not all yarns in the same weight give the same result. For example, there are enormous differences in the DK yarns used in these patterns. You need to consider the recommended tension or gauge instructions and the length of the skein. I have found the www.yarnsub.com website wonderful for finding substitute yarns in the past. But if you can, try using the same yarns I have. You won't regret it.

AUSTRALIAN COUNTRY SPINNERS
(www.auspinners.com.au)

With a history going back to the early twentieth century, Australian Country Spinners produces famous Australian brands such as Patons, Cleckheaton, Panda and Shepherd. I have used some of their premium Australian merino yarns.

Cleckheaton Australian Superfine Merino DK

100% superfine merino

Skein: 2.29 oz (65 g), 142 yds (130 m)

Gauge: 22 stitches per 4 in (10 cm)

Recommended needles: US 6 (4 mm)

Used in: Go Anywhere Woman's Vest (page 11)

Cleckheaton Country Merino 8 ply

100% Australian merino

Skein: 1.76 oz (50 g), 94 yds (86 m)

Gauge: 22 stitches per 4 in (10 cm)

Recommended needles: US 2–3 (2.75–3.25 mm)

Used in: Houndstooth Vest (page 99)

Patons Dreamtime Merino 4 ply

100% merino

Skein: 1.76 oz (50 g), 185 yds (169 m)

Gauge: 28 stitches per 4 in (10 cm)

Recommended needles: US 3 (3.25 mm)

Used in: Classic Weave Scarf (page 48)

LION BRAND YARNS

(www.lionbrand.com)

One of the USA's oldest yarn-crafting companies — they were established in 1878 and provide a total online solution for yarn-crafters. They have patterns (many are free), yarn, needles, hooks and accessories. I have used two yarns from their premium LB Collection and used them in many projects.

LB Collection Angora Merino DK

80% extrafine merino, 20% angora

Skein: 1.76 oz (50 g), 131 yds (120 m)

Gauge: 20 stitches per 4 in (10 cm)

Recommended needles: US 7 (4.5 mm)

Used in: Women's Shaped Vest (page 41)

LB Collection Superwash Merino 8 ply

100% superwash merino

Skein: 3.5 oz (100 g), 306 yds (280 m)

Gauge: 22 stitches per 4 in (10 cm)

Recommended needles: US 6 (4 mm)

Used in: Square Play Reversible Hat (page 72), Catch a Star Vest (page 61), Winter Warmth Mittens (page 69) and Simple Striped Fingerless Gloves (page 45)

NATURALLY YARNS

(www.naturallyyarnsnz.com)

Producing fine New Zealand yarns since the 1980s, Naturally Yarns is now part of a large Italian yarn company that sells many famous brands internationally. I have used a selection of their New Zealand merino yarns.

Baby Natural DK

100% New Zealand rare breed Arapawa merino

Skein: 1.76 oz (50 g), 165 yds (151 m)

Gauge: 22 stitches per 4 in (10 cm)

Recommended needles: US 3–6 (3.25–4 mm)

Used in: Cozy Hat (page 65)

Harmony 10 ply

100% New Zealand merino

Skein: 1.76 oz (50 g), 116 yds (106 m)

Gauge: 20 stitches per 4 in (10 cm)

Recommended needles: US 6–8 (4–5 mm)

Used in: Cozy Hat (page 65)

Harmony Colour DK

100% pure New Zealand Merino

Skein: 1.76 oz (50 g), 145 yds (159 m)

Gauge: 22 stitches per 4 in (10 cm)

Recommended needles: US 3–6 (3.25–4 mm)

Used in: Woman's Cable Vest (page 82)

Merino/Silk DK

70% merino, 20% silk, 10% nylon

Skein: 1.76 oz (50 g), 137 yds (150 m)

Gauge: 20–22 stitches per 4 in (10 cm)

Recommended needles: US 3–6 (3.25–4 mm)

Used in: Woman's Cable Vest (page 82)

Waikiwi 4 ply

55% merino, 20% nylon, 15% alpaca, 10% possum

Skein: 1.76 oz (50 g), 198 yds (181 m)

Gauge: 22 stitches per 4 in (10 cm)

Recommended needles: US 2–3 (2.75–3.25 mm)

Used in: Cabled Fingerless Gloves (page 55), Reversible Mosaic Hat (page 51), Winter Fire Scarf (page 91) and Winter Fire Beanie (page 89)

Waikiwi Prints 4 ply

55% merino, 20% nylon, 15% alpaca, 10% possum

Skein: 1.76 oz (50 g), 198 yds (181 m)

Gauge: 22 stitches per 4 in (10 cm)

Recommended needles: US 2–3 (2.75–3.25 mm)

Used in: Classic Weave Scarf (page 48), Reversible Mosaic Hat (page 51), Winter Fire Scarf (page 91) and Winter Fire Beanie (page 89)

THE RARE YARNS COMPANY
(www.rareyarns.co.nz)

Rare Yarns is a boutique New Zealand yarn company that approaches their business believing that 'people are passionate about yarns that are beautiful, out of the ordinary and lovely to touch' and I could not agree more. Of course I have chosen merino blends from their range, but each yarn is so very different in structure, weight and color.

Tree Children DK

80% alpaca, 20% merino

Skein: 1.76 oz (50 g), 110 yds (10 m)

Gauge: 22 stitches per 4 in (10 cm)

Recommended needles: US 6 (4 mm)

Used in: Cabled Beanie (page 105)

Rare Fire Brushed 14 ply

50% alpaca, 30% mohair and 20% superfine merino

Skein: 1.76 oz (50 g), 87 yards (80 m)

Gauge: 13 stitches per 4 in (10 cm)

Recommended needles: US 10.5–11 (6.5–8 mm)

Used in: Long Scarf (page 121)

Rotoiti Alpaca Merino 10 ply

80% alpaca, 20% merino

Skein: 1.75 oz (50 g), 97 yds (88.5 m)

Gauge: 19 stitches per 4 in (10 cm)

Recommended needles: US 7 (4.5 mm)

Used in: Slouch Vest (page 31)

SKEINZ
(www.skeinz.com)

Skeinz runs its own mill and sells directly to the public. They offer premium spun yarns at reasonable prices through their retail and online shop. I love the feel of these yarns as you knit, and the finished work as well.

Burlesque DK

75% merino, 25% tussah silk

Skein: 1.76 oz (50 g), 106 yds (96 m)

Gauge: 22 stitches per 4 in (10 cm)

Recommended needles: US 6 (4 mm)

Used in Slouch Beanie (page 85)

Skeinz Heritage Silver Lining 8 ply

Pure New Zealand rare fine breed 100% merino yarn

Skein: 1.76 oz (50 g), 119 yds (109 m)

Gauge: 20–22 stitches per 4 in (10 cm)

Recommended needles: US 6 (4 mm)

Used in: Fingerless Fair Isle Gloves (page 96), Weekend Khaki Vest (page 23) and All Natural Cabled Beanie (page 76)

TOUCH YARNS
(www.touchyarns.com)

Touch Yarns uses the by-line 'The Beautiful Yarn Company' and this family-run business is not wrong. Touch Yarns' hand-dyed merino/possum yarns are individual works of art and, when knitted, have the same individuality about them.

Hand-Dyed Possum Merino DK

60% merino, 30% possum, 10% silk

Skein: 3.5 oz (100 g), 460 yds (420 m)

Gauge: 28 stitches per 4 in (10 cm)

Recommended needles: US 5 (3.75 mm)

Used in All Weather Vest (page 111)

Pure Merino 8 ply/DK

100% merino yarn

Skein: 1.76 oz (50 g), 109 yds (100 m)

Gauge: 22 stitches per 4 in (10 cm)

Recommended needles: US 6 (4 mm)

Used in: Infinite Diamonds Scarf (page 13)

ZEALANA YARNS
(www.zealana.com)

Zealana, based in New Zealand, creates luxurious yarns that feature brushtail possum fiber. Possums are declared pests in New Zealand and their fiber is soft and light and adds warmth without heaviness to yarn mixes.

Zealana Artisan Cozi 4 ply

58% merino, 20% nylon, 15% possum, 5% alpaca, 2% elastic nylon

Skein: 1.76 oz (50 g), 186 yds (170 m)

Gauge: 28–40 stitches per 4 in (10 cm)

Recommended needles: US 1 (2.25 mm)

Used in: Chevron Beanie (page 19)

Zealana Artisan Series Heron worsted weight

80% fine merino, 20% brushtail possum yarn

Skein: 1.76 oz (50 g), 109 yds (100 m)

Gauge: 18–20 stitches per 4 in (10 cm)

Recommended needles: US 6–8 (4–5 mm)

Used in: Sou'wester Hat (page 35) and Rugged Fingerless Gloves (page 16)

Zealana Kauri worsted weight

60% merino, 30% brushtail possum, 10% mulberry silk

Skein: 1.76 oz (50 g), 94 yds (86 m)

Gauge: 20 stitches per 4 in (10 cm)

Recommended needles: US 7 (4.5 mm)

Used in: Warm Woodsman Hat (page 27), Nature's Stripes Scarf (page 108) and Sleeveless Hoodie (page 115)

In addition to the yarns above, I also used some generic 4-ply merino yarns for the Zig-Zag Scarf (page 79).

STANDARD YARN WEIGHT SYSTEM

Categories of yarn, gauge ranges and recommended needle sizes.
Source: Craft Yarn Council www.YarnStandards.com

YARN WEIGHT SYMBOL & CATEGORY NAMES	TYPE OF YARNS IN CATEGORY	KNIT GAUGE* IN ST. ST TO 4 IN (10 CM)	RECOMMENDED METRIC NEEDLE SIZE	RECOMMENDED US NEEDLE SIZE
1 SUPER FINE	Sock, Fingering, Baby	27–32 sts	2.25–3.25 mm	1–3
2 FINE	Sport, Baby	23–26 sts	3.25–3.75 mm	3–5
3 LIGHT	DK, Light Worsted	21–24 st	3.75–4.5 mm	5–7
4 MEDIUM	Worsted, Afghan, Aran	16–20 sts	4.5–5.5 mm	7–9
5 BULKY	Chunky, Craft, Rug	12–15 sts	5.5–8 mm	9–11

*Guidelines only: the above reflect the most commonly used gauges and needle sizes for specific yarn categories.

NOTE: In Australia, New Zealand and the UK, 'ply' is often used to describe the weight (thickness) of a yarn, as follows:

4 ply	Sock, Baby
5 ply	Sport, Baby
8 ply	DK, Light worsted
10 ply	Worsted, Afghan, Aran
12 ply	Chunky, Craft, Rug